Rebekah Baggs and Chris Corak

SEO FOR EVERYONE

MORE FROM A BOOK APART

Visit abookapart.com for our full list of titles.

Publisher: Jeffrey Zeldman
Designer: Jason Santa Maria
Executive director: Katel LeDû
Managing editor: Lisa Maria Marquis
Editors: Sally Kerrigan, Caren Litherland, Christopher Hagge
Technical editor: Mat Marquis
Technical reviewers: Dana DiTomaso, Mike Corak
Book producer: Ron Bilodeau

ISBN: 978-1-952616-07-5

A Book Apart
New York, New York
http://abookapart.com

10 9 8 7 6 5 4 3 2 1

TABLE OF CONTENTS

FOREWORD

I USED TO HATE SEO. All those nefarious practices to lure people to websites just for the sake of *traffic*! For years, I sat through presentations by SEO companies who promised me that they could get me to the number-one spot on Google rankings, that I'd beat all the competition. All I had to do was produce content. Lots of content. Lots and *lots* of content, with lots and lots of words, on lots and lots of topics.

Did my organization have anything at all to do with these topics? No. Did we have to maintain all of this new content, at a cost? Yes. Did the content get us traffic? Sure.

Was it traffic that was actually of use to us or to our audience? No.

And there we have it. The real problem.

I went to Rebekah and Chris's presentation at Confab Central 2019, expecting to confirm my view that SEO is nothing more than vanity metrics and money, always in conflict with the user experience. And I was so wrong. I came away from their talk with love and admiration. Their approach to SEO was leagues ahead of the global companies we'd worked with. They talked about search with flair, passion, and expertise. They suggested easy, practical tasks I could share with my clients immediately—tasks that would unify content and search rather than pitting them against each other.

Now they have put this mesmerizing information into a book for us. Handy. Thank you, Rebekah and Chris.

This isn't a book about how to game the rankings system. This is a book about long-lasting relevance to your audience. It's about producing good content. It is a thorough, in-depth look at how to rank well in search by serving your users and becoming brand champions. In short, it's the only book on SEO I'd recommend.

Optimize for the humans. Let the tech do the rest.

—Sarah Winters

INTRODUCTION

SEARCH ENGINE OPTIMIZATION (SEO) is the practice of earning visibility in search engine results to increase both the quantity and quality of organic traffic to a website. Many web professionals view SEO as a function of marketing.

But SEO is about so much more than marketing. It's about discovery. It's about accessibility. It's about helping people find the information they need to make important decisions.

Addressing search in digital projects deserves a thoughtful approach that focuses on meeting user needs and delivering a better experience—what we call *human-centered SEO*. And because it requires a deep understanding of your audiences, their needs and priorities, and, more importantly, what they're trying to accomplish on your site, this kind of SEO needs to be *part* of the overall design strategy, not the final step.

Human-centered SEO as design

Human-centered SEO requires design, content, and code decisions to be made in harmony. You can't sprinkle SEO magic on polished web copy just before hitting publish and expect your site to rank well in search, or actually meet the search needs of real people.

In fact, that would be an impossible task: a lot of critical SEO elements—like content topics, navigation labels, and internal linking structures—are built into early design decisions. A lot of SEO work looks exactly like design, content, and development work—*because it is.*

Unfortunately, search optimization is often an afterthought in most web design workflows—a cursory task that comes after all the research, user experience design, and sometimes even writing is done. SEO can even be a source of conflict and bad feelings because of its unethical, spammy history. At best, SEO is seen as pushy marketing tactics that chase vanity metrics; at worst, it can feel completely at odds with a good user experience.

But it doesn't have to be that way.

Human-centered SEO shifts the focus from "How much traffic can we win?" to "How can we help more people find what they're looking for?" It emphasizes satisfying search intent—the actual task, question, or problem that drives the user to search for something in the first place. This shift changes everything, and makes you—yes, you, dear reader—part of the equation.

SEO is your job, too

SEO isn't the unwieldy monster it's made out to be, relegated to a dark, spooky corner of the design process. It just needs a bit of understanding, some cross-disciplinary collaboration, and a little TLC.

Want to know a secret about people with "SEO" in their job title? They don't actually implement every possible aspect of search optimization. They may guide decisions that benefit findability. They may make recommendations about how to craft content for search visibility. Or they may ensure important technical factors aren't overlooked during development.

But when it comes to optimizing any website, there's still plenty of necessity for people like you—the designers, content specialists, developers, and project managers of the world—to get involved. Most web professionals are, at heart, communicators; and most SEO challenges are, at heart, communication challenges.

Optimizing search isn't about using the right tools or knowing the best techniques—it's about understanding the role of search in delivering the best possible user experience. You are an essential part of making human-centered SEO happen.

What to expect

In this book, we aren't going to teach you everything there is to know about SEO, and this book can't take the place of working with an SEO specialist. Having help from a seasoned search professional is a good idea on any web project, especially if your organization is large and complex.

But we *will* show you exactly where SEO and design intersect, and help you identify the tools and techniques you need to create content that's both user-friendly and search-friendly. Whether you're completely new to SEO or a bona fide search professional yourself, our mission is to give you the insights you need to successfully collaborate across teams and disciplines and integrate SEO into your design process.

Let's explore some practical ways to do just that.

1
MODERN SEARCH

SEO IS PART OF DESIGN, and design is part of SEO—and the evolution of search shows us why. You don't need to know every detail of SEO's history to integrate search standards into your design process, but a little context will help a lot. We promise.

We'll start off by defining what SEO is (and isn't) and describing how search engines work, and then walk through the history of search algorithms and ranking factors. Finally, we'll talk about the process Google uses so we can better understand how design, content, and UX impact the search experience—and ultimately how much visibility your site merits.

THE PRACTICE OF SEO

Most user experiences don't start on our carefully designed websites, but on a list of Google search results. In fact, over half of all website traffic comes from organic search, which means that SEO, for better or worse, is part of a user's overall experience of a site (http://bkaprt.com/seo38/01-01).

While its name might imply that we're optimizing for search engines, that's only half of the story. The practice of SEO is as much about understanding people—the tasks they want to accomplish, the questions they have, the problems they're trying to solve, and the language they use to describe things—as it is about making sure web crawlers (the kind that read web pages and organize them into a search index) can find and understand your content.

Optimization can take myriad forms, many of which fall into more than one category. To keep things simple, we'll say SEO primarily affects the following five areas:

- **Content:** Looking at the subject, quality, clarity, accuracy, and depth of content, along with meta descriptions, alt text, keywords, and alignment with search intent.
- **Information architecture:** Aligning content organization, categorization, hierarchy, and labeling with search intent, keywords, and the language people use to describe what they're looking for.
- **User experience:** Focusing on the features and functionality of the content, its ease of use and access, and its ability to satisfy search intent.
- **Code:** Addressing site speed, XML sitemaps, canonical links, `robots.txt` files, pagination, site migrations and redirect strategies, SSL and HTTPS standards, and more.
- **Authority:** Working with internal link-building, inbound links, brand reputation, marketing, credibility, reviews, social proof, and other trust factors.

And within these five areas, there's a lot of subject matter to cover and gain expertise around. That's why, much like the disciplines of user experience design or content strategy, SEO has different areas of focus, each with its own set of goals:

- **Onsite:** Optimizing web pages through information architecture, site design, usability, and the satisfaction of search intent in core web content. Most of this book will focus on this type of SEO.
- **Technical:** Developing websites with indexing, structured data implementation, CMS functionality, and security in mind. We'll touch on this just enough to give you the tools

to either code and build in a search-friendly way, or work effectively with developers.

- **Editorial:** Researching and identifying opportunities for content creation and content marketing. Editorial SEO uses a lot of the same techniques as onsite SEO, but with the goal of generating ongoing content.
- **Local:** Increasing visibility in organic searches for brick-and-mortar businesses. This emphasizes business listings, citations (online mentions) and contact details, and service areas and hours of operation (like "late-night coffee shops open now near me" or "24-hour urgent care"). We won't cover this area much at all.
- **Off-site:** Strengthening relationships and influence with other websites and earning legitimate *backlinks* (inbound links to your site from other authoritative websites). Think of this as the public relations side of SEO. We won't cover this area either.

It's unusual to find someone who excels at every kind of SEO. Although there are a few unicorns out there, most professionals worth their salt will specialize in just one or two areas. If you're working with consultants or adding an SEO professional to your team, make sure their strengths align with the kind of work you're trying to do, or work with an agency that has a team of experts across the spectrum.

MYTHBUSTING SEO

Even though you now have a picture of what the general practice of SEO looks like, you're probably still wondering what exactly SEO can and can't do. There are a lot of misconceptions around that, so let's clear them up!

SEO *can*:

- make it easier for users to search for specific answers, information, products, or services you're offering;
- help people find the content that's most relevant to their geographic location or the language they're searching in;

- help you leverage search data to improve user experiences and content;
- make your search listing stand out, feel more compelling, and provide users with a reason to click; and
- enable your content to be featured by Google in answer boxes, featured snippets, and other desirable formats.

SEO *cannot*:

- work overnight (it's a long-term play);
- guarantee your site will be highly ranked in search results or used in any Google-controlled features, like answer boxes or featured snippets;
- get content on sites that lack domain or brand authority (like new microsites or sites built on subdomains) to rank highly in search results; or
- bring in lots of traffic for a product or service no one really needs, a problem no one really has, or anything people aren't searching for in the first place.

GOOGLE SETS THE BAR

Google is the standard for how we frame search, its evolution, and where things stand today. It's the only search engine that really matters in SEO. Are there search engines besides Google? Sure. Baidu is important if you're doing SEO for mainland China. Yandex is important if you're optimizing for visibility in Russia. Does anyone still use Bing? Possibly. But with more than 90 percent of the search market share worldwide at the time of writing, Google easily represents the majority of users (http://bkaprt.com/seo38/01-02, http://bkaprt.com/seo38/01-03).

So Google doesn't just *lead* the search market share—it dominates it. Google sets the standard for search algorithm development, as well as crawling and indexing technology (i.e., how search engines work). Therefore, we'll focus on how SEO has evolved under Google's leadership and the search standards the company has set. Now that we've gotten that out of the way, let's dive in.

WHAT SEARCH ENGINES DO

In its *Beginners Guide to SEO* (which we highly recommend to anyone who wants to get a more comprehensive overview of SEO basics), SEO software and data company Moz says that search engines "exist to discover, understand, and organize the internet's content in order to offer the most relevant results to the questions searchers are asking" (http://bkaprt.com/seo38/01-04).

To do this, search engines have four main directives (**FIG 1.1**):

- **Crawling.** Search engine bots crawl the web looking for as many URLs as they can find, and scan everything including page titles, images, keywords, code, and other linked pages. Errors in your metatags or `robot.txt` files (a text file that tells a search engine where you want (and don't want) them to crawl on your site), or technology that isn't search engine-friendly, can prevent search engines from being able to see and index your content.
- **Indexing.** After the search engine discovers your content in its crawl, it determines what your content is about (through semantic relevance and other factors), and then organizes and stores that content in a process called *indexing*. When people search Google, they're not really searching the web—they're searching Google's database of crawled content.
- **Ranking.** Once your web pages are indexed, they'll be shown in the *search engine results page* (SERP) when people make relevant queries. The algorithm takes many ranking signals into consideration to determine your content's relevance to the search query. Organic results are then ordered from most to least relevant, under the paid results at the very top. (Keep in mind that whatever you may be doing in paid search has no effect whatsoever on your organic rankings.)
- **Post-rank assessment.** After your content is initially ranked, Google continuously evaluates how people interact with your page to monitor and adjust the quality of the ranking, if necessary. If Google sees any feedback signal or indication that a page isn't satisfying the searcher's intent or answering their question (for example, if people quickly abandon your

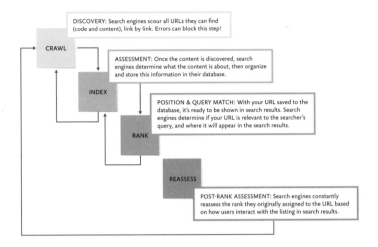

FIG 1.1: All search engines work in essentially the same way: crawling the web to find URLs, indexing and assessing the content, and finally assigning search rankings. These rankings are continually refined based on how users interact with a page after clicking on the search listing.

page and return to the search engine or skip your search listing for a lower-ranking one), it tries to find a more relevant result to move higher on the SERP.

HOW SEO EARNED A BAD REPUTATION

Google cares about giving people what they want. Even its webmaster guidelines on optimizing for search suggests asking yourself: "Does this help my users? Would I do this if search engines didn't exist?" (http://bkaprt.com/seo38/01-05)

So why did anyone ever try to game the system? Well, for a while there, gaming algorithms was just plain *easier* than meeting peoples' needs—and it worked. Early on, Google relied on overly simple ranking factors like keyword matching to indicate relevance, and backlink volume to indicate value. If a lot of people are linking to a site, then it *must* be good, right?

But this ranking system was pretty easy to manipulate. Google's early algorithms weren't sophisticated enough to take quality and legitimacy into account—so with a little strategic keyword stuffing and some backlinks from fake sites, you could be well on your way to appearing on the first page of Google search results!

Back then, leveraging those loopholes in search algorithms became commonplace. But it was only a matter of time until Google figured out how to reinstate order amid the chaos.

HOW ALGORITHMS EVOLVED TO SET THINGS RIGHT

SEO has changed a lot since its spammy early days, and Google has worked hard to codify the complexity of human search behavior. They've gradually built a smarter, more sophisticated search algorithm with the power to deliver meaningful, valuable, and relevant results.

Keep in mind that *nobody but Google* really knows the details of how their search algorithm works; it's a highly guarded secret. To discourage people from trying to game the system, exact ranking factors aren't disclosed.

However, Google does give us a lot of clues through their guidelines and best-practices documentation. It's safe to say that the algorithm looks at:

- content quality,
- legitimate links and authority,
- relevance,
- search intent, and
- user experience.

Thankfully, the SEO community has run myriad tests to try to suss out which factors matter more than others, and our own experience has shown us what kind of site improvements really move the needle. We can use that collective knowledge to get a better understanding of how to optimize for relevant factors. Here's a deeper look into what we know matters.

Content quality

Quality can be complex and subjective. It's even more challenging to assess algorithmically, though Google tries. Of course, Google does not disclose the specifics of how they assess content quality, but they do offer writing guidelines that place a lot of focus on factors like trustworthiness, quality control, and alignment with readers' genuine interests (http://bkaprt.com/seo38/01-06).

Legitimate links and authority

Think of links to your site from other sites as weighted votes. A link from a large, well-known, and respected site counts for a lot, while a link from a lesser-known site counts just a little. In aggregate, links help determine how authoritative your content is and exert a positive influence on how Google sees your site's value.

But as we said earlier, this kind of system used to be easy to manipulate. After they adjusted the algorithm to home in on quality, Google turned its attention to filtering out sites engaging in fake link-building and keyword-stuffing practices. And, holy shit, was there ever a mountain of garbage to clean up. These days, you've got to *earn* your links if you want them to count.

Relevance

In 2013, Google released a significant algorithm update (more like an overhaul) called Hummingbird, which put greater emphasis on natural-language queries, focusing on context and meaning over individual keywords. It drastically improved the search engine's semantic understanding of the web and how topics of information relate or connect to one another.

Hummingbird focused on synonyms and theme-related topics, so *exact-match* (meaning exactly the same word for word) keywords don't matter as much as much as they used to. Google shows results that are relevant to the search, rather than only the searcher's keywords. That means you don't have to know the one correct phrase to match user queries, as long as you're using semantically relevant language and navigation labels to clearly communicate your content.

Search intent

Following the Hummingbird update, Google made further refinements to their natural-language processing capabilities with a machine-learning artificial intelligence system called RankBrain, which continuously "teaches" Google how to understand semantics better.

More recently, Google implemented BERT, which stands for *Bidirectional Encoder Representations from Transformers*. BERT uses natural language processing (NLP) to understand not only nuances in words' meanings, but also how meanings change when words are used together (http://bkaprt.com/seo38/01-07). It's one of the biggest steps forward in the history of search.

You can see these advancements at work when you search for something like "Italian plumbers." Previously, you might get an actual listing of plumbers in Italy, but now (unless you are performing this search in Italian while located in Italy), Google understands that you probably aren't looking for plumbers— you're searching for video game characters. Because BERT can understand these nuances, Google shows images of Mario and Luigi (**FIG 1.2**).

Google understands what searchers want and need—it understands their *intent*. That's a big deal, and it means that doing the work to understand and address search intent on your site is incredibly important.

FIG 1.2: The search engine results page for "Italian plumbers" shows how Google is able to extrapolate intent from search queries and deliver contextually relevant results.

User experience

Design—including the content, code, and interface—matters in SEO because design shapes how users behave. Most SEO professionals believe Google assesses a site's user experience by incorporating behavioral data in its ranking systems. As we've mentioned, Google keeps its *exact* use of behavioral data secret, but these are likely factors:

- **Click-through rate:** How many clicks a search listing receives in relation to how many times it is shown.
- **Pogo-sticking:** Returning to the search results for a different page. This implies that the first page didn't satisfy the user's intent, or the experience didn't meet their expectations (because of slow loading times, say, or being hard to use on a mobile device).
- **Dwell time:** The amount of time a user spends on a page before returning to Google.
- **Real-life behavior:** Geopositioning a user's physical location (via mobile apps) to see if they actually visit a place they searched for.
- **Mobile experience:** How your site is viewed on small screens and devices. Google's change to mobile-first indexing determines your rankings for *all* screen sizes, even desktop (http://bkaprt.com/seo38/01-08).

Whether these signals are being used as direct ranking factors, feedback to train the algorithm, or something else entirely is unclear. But most SEO practitioners recognize that Google is analyzing some level of user satisfaction to ensure it sends users the most appropriate results.

No matter how the algorithm has evolved, one theme stands out: search intent matters. In a comparison of Google's ranking signals from 2014 to 2019, Rand Fishkin, cofounder and CEO of SparkToro and formerly of Moz, demonstrated that intent had moved from the sixth most critical ranking factor all the way up to number one (**FIG 1.3**).

Furthermore, there's a theme with all the ranking factors that now carry more weight in the algorithm, like *intent matching, content structure, comprehensiveness,* and *content accuracy*: they're user-centric. As Google becomes more sophisticated in understanding what users are looking for, along with gaining a better understanding of the meaning of our content, *people* have become more important. At the same time, purely technical ranking factors that can be easily manipulated and have less of an impact on user experience, like *keyword matching* and *inbound anchor text*, have declined.

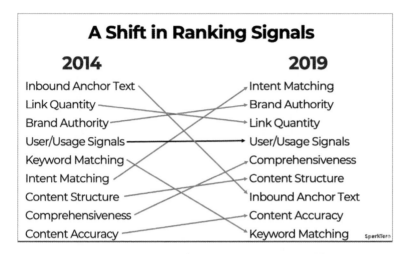

FIG 1.3: This slide from Rand Fishkin's keynote at MozCon 2019 shows how much ranking signals have pivoted to focus on user experience since 2014. Image courtesy of Rand Fishkin.

WHAT DOES IT ALL MEAN?

This evolution of search algorithms means that what Google really wants is for you to make pages primarily for *users,* not search engines! It wants you to avoid tricks intended to improve search engine rankings and do the hard work required to provide a good user experience.

It also means that one of the most important things you can do to improve search visibility for your site is to satisfy search intent—to think about why someone would come to your site in the first place, and ensure their expectations are met. In the next chapter, we'll take a closer look at what search intent is and how you can uncover it on your own.

2 UNDERSTANDING SEARCH INTENT

" Search intent is of fundamental importance. You just can't compete in the long term, or even the short term, if you don't serve intent better than your competitors on the first page of search results. The content on your page and the experience that your website provides must serve what the user is seeking, or someone else will take that ranking position from you.
—RAND FISHKIN, IN DISCUSSION WITH THE AUTHORS, AUGUST 2019

WHEN SOMEONE CLICKS THROUGH to your page from a search result, the thing they came to do is known as their *search intent*. It's the task the user is looking to accomplish, the problem they're trying to solve, or the information they hope to learn when they turn to a search engine. If their experience on your site doesn't align with those expectations, users will likely return to the search results to find a site that *will* satisfy their intent.

When you analyze search intent, you not only discover what tasks people are trying to accomplish, but also how they search, what topics they care about, and what language they use to describe things. Understanding search intent is the most critical component of creating a human-centered SEO strategy. It's what aligns SEO and design in a user-friendly way.

THE BENEFITS OF UNDERSTANDING SEARCH INTENT

Both Google and Bing have stated that anyone practicing SEO also needs to understand how to research and design for search intent (http://bkaprt.com/seo38/02-01). Satisfying search intent not only impacts search performance (by improving visibility and conversions, for example), but also enhances a site's overall user experience. It ensures that you're answering questions that otherwise would have remained unanswered on your site, and that you're helping users solve problems.

Studying search intent is probably one of the most underutilized forms of user research. Content writers and UX professionals are at an advantage here, because they're already pretty ace at trying to understand what users want—and when they satisfy search intent, their content can provide even more value to users.

A better understanding of user needs

Much like interviews or journey mapping, search intent analysis is a form of research you can lean on to better understand user needs. But since this type of research is based on numbers and stats, you'll gain the formidable power of quantifiable data to back up your decision-making.

Search intent is uncovered by mining deep sets of search data and studying search result pages, a practice we refer to as *search intent analysis*. This might sound a bit like keyword research, which is typically used to identify the most common or popular terms and phrases searchers are using, with a view toward incorporating them into your content. But it's not the same thing.

Search intent analysis is a more user-centered way to look at search data. As Dan Shure, SEO consultant at Evolving SEO and host of the podcast *Experts on the Wire,* says: "Search volume isn't a number you look at to see how much traffic you can 'get,' it's how many people a month you can help with whatever they are asking" (http://bkaprt.com/seo38/02-02). In other words, how can you design an experience that gives users the information they're looking for? By prioritizing user needs rather than increased search visibility, your site has the best shot at earning that visibility (and without any extra work on your part).

Understanding search data isn't just a marketing opportunity. It shows you that real people are behind every single search, trying to find answers to real-life questions. *You* can help them.

More context for qualitative research

The most common forms of user research—like user interviews—can produce excellent qualitative insights, but they lack quantitative support. Content and UX folks often look for numbers to help validate discovered themes and lend rigor to their qualitative research. That's where search data comes in.

Estimated *search volume*—real numbers that represent real people—is crucial to backing up your findings. Search intent research can help identify content opportunities and prioritization, as well as quantify risks—all while being composed of data-driven, fact-based numbers that are indisputable.

Quicker, easier, cheaper research

Many forms of user research require extensive planning, coordination, and budget. Segmenting audiences, scheduling interviews, and hosting journey-mapping sessions are a lot of work. It's not always easy to incentivize and inspire participation in research studies, much less get budget approved to pay for it. These hurdles stack up fast, often extending timelines or, even worse, blocking research from happening at all.

But search intent analysis doesn't require the same level of planning, nor is it as costly. Search data is accessible to anyone (limited access is generally free, and deeper access is inexpensive) at any time (you can start your research now, this very minute).

Although the insight you glean from search intent data is always improved by pairing it with user interviews, search intent research is worthwhile even on its own. And getting started doesn't require coordination with users: to access raw search data from everyone in the world, all you need is a login to a keyword tool.

GOOGLE'S BROAD CATEGORIES OF INTENT

Back in 2002, in an internal document called "A Taxonomy of Web Search," Andrei Broder, then vice president of research at AltaVista, wrote that search intent can be categorized into three different types (http://bkaprt.com/seo38/02-03, PDF):

- **Informational.** The user wants to learn about a topic. Informational searches might look like:
    - "is life insurance tax deductible"
    - "how long do running shoes last"
    - "income tax brackets"
    - "fender jaguar vs jazzmaster"

- **Transactional.** The user wants to take action—to make a purchase, say, or download a product manual. Transactional search intent is not always tied to buying something. Transactional searches might look like:
    - "life insurance quotes"
    - "fugazi in on the kill taker on vinyl"
    - "RACI chart template"

- **Navigational.** With this kind of search, someone wants to go to a specific website or find a specific page (perhaps one they've visited before). There's typically only one destination the searcher is trying to get to. Navigational searches look like:
    - "aflac claims"
    - "amazon.com"
    - "powell books"
    - "wikipedia life insurance"
    - "healthline keto diet"

Google later adopted and repurposed these classifications as *Know*, *Do*, and *Website*, and added a fourth category, *Visit-in-person* (http://bkaprt.com/seo38/02-04, PDF):

- **Visit-in-person.** These searches have local, real-world intent; someone is seeking an in-person experience or a brick-and-mortar interaction. Visit-in-person searches look like this:
  - "insurance agent in phoenix"
  - "thai restaurants open now"
  - "movie times"
  - "barber shops"
  - "discount tire near me"

One of the ways Google utilizes these four types of intent is in the design of its search engine results pages, or SERPs. The classification of intent determines what SERP features appear in order to provide more relevant results. For example, for queries identified with informational intent, Google may insert a featured snippet or how-to video. If it identifies transactional intent, it may display ranking product pages or product listing ads, or guide users to retailers. When visit-in-person intent is recognized, Google inserts business listings with a map or localizes other results to guide people to nearby resources.

Note that in the real world, while some searches fall into a single classification, many fall into multiple areas of intent. A user searching for "the perfect pour over" could be attempting to learn about the best method for making a pour-over cup of coffee, or they could be thinking about buying a setup that makes a great cup. Google recognizes both possibilities (**FIG 2.1**): informational intent (as evidenced by the featured snippet and video results), and transactional intent (as seen in the product listing ads). It tries to deliver the right answer as quickly as possible, saving the user from having to conduct multiple follow-up searches.

While these high-level classifications are great for understanding the general form of search intent and what kind of rich results and SERP features you should optimize for, they don't specifically address what the user's needs are, or the insights required to make design and content decisions that

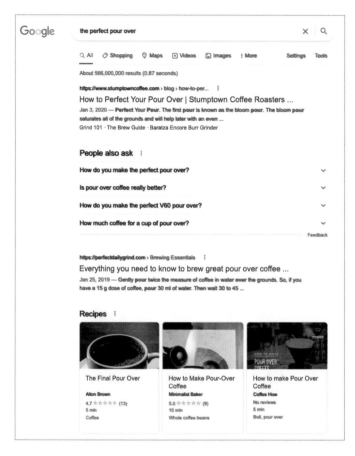

FIG 2.1: By showing search results for multiple forms of intent, Google reduces the likelihood that users will have to conduct more specific follow-up searches.

will allow you to earn visibility. It's not enough to understand that someone wants to make a transaction; you also have to understand what type of information people need in order to feel comfortable making the transaction in the first place. Uncovering these nuanced search needs equips you with the insights to design experiences that truly satisfy the searcher's intent, and in turn earn visibility.

ANALYZING THE SERP

The best way to start researching search intent is by analyzing the SERP for the most popular keywords and phrases around your product, service, or subject matter. The SERP can be made up of many different types of content and data elements, and which elements appear for a given query provide clues as to how Google assesses the user's search intent.

Take, for example, the SERP for the term "life insurance" (**FIG 2.2**). SERP features on this page include:

- Ad listings (ignore these)
- Blue links with information on cost and quotes
- A knowledge panel with a basic definition
- A "People also ask" box with information on the different types of life insurance

The elements of the SERP provide clear evidence of search intent around the topic of life insurance. Google calculates that users searching for "life insurance" generally want to learn more about what life insurance is and how it works, to find out what kind of plan is right for them, and to get a feel for how much it'll cost. Various SERP features are presented to try to satisfy that intent.

To get started, choose a search query that's relevant to your product or industry, and jot down all of the content ideas, topics, and indicators of intent you can find on the SERP. Be sure to ignore any ads; since someone paid for them to be there, they might not reflect actual search intent. At the end of this process, you'll have a list of search intent ideas related to your topic, which you can use to assess your current content and generate new content.

Note that many different features may appear on a SERP, though they won't all appear on every SERP; it depends on which features Google thinks will be most useful for your query. Let's dig into the SERP features that are most useful for studying search intent:

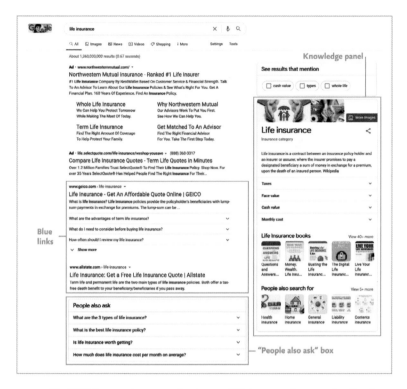

FIG 2.2: The SERP features that appear for the term "life insurance" suggest that Google determines this search query as driven by primarily information and transactional intent.

- Blue links
- "People also ask" boxes
- Local packs
- "People also search for" and "Related searches" boxes
- Knowledge panels
- Predictive search dropdowns

Blue links

Blue links are the basic organic results of your search. Over the years, Google's SERP has evolved to display all kinds of rich search components, from featured snippets to embedded

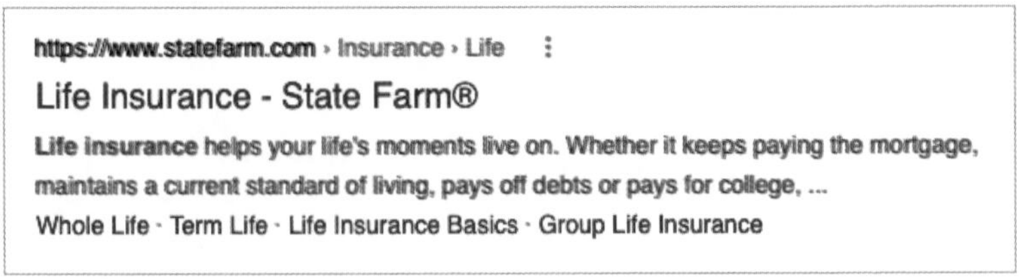

https://www.statefarm.com › Insurance › Life ⋮

Life Insurance - State Farm®

Life insurance helps your life's moments live on. Whether it keeps paying the mortgage, maintains a current standard of living, pays off debts or pays for college, ...

Whole Life · Term Life · Life Insurance Basics · Group Life Insurance

FIG 2.3: The four blue links under the main search listing indicate what Google thinks users will want to do next.

video—yet the staple of the search results page has always been blue links.

Here's what you'll want to look for:

- **What sites appear, and what insights do they provide?** If you search for "life insurance," you might see third-party review sites, life insurance providers, and educational content publishers—which means Google thinks users want unbiased reviews to help them find the best life insurance, suggestions for where to shop, and information on how to make smart decisions about their purchase.
- **What language is used in each link?** Do a quick search for "life insurance" and check out the headlines of each result. You'll see blue link titles with phrases like "types of policies," "best life insurance providers," and "whole life insurance." The headlines offer another clue about how Google synthesizes the search intent. In this case, we see a combined search intent: transactional intent (terms like "whole life insurance" signal that someone is shopping around for plans) is mixed in with informational intent (indicated by phrases like "policy types" and "best providers").
- **What do the organic site links point to?** Sometimes, underneath a site listing, you'll see several other smaller links below the meta description (**FIG 2.3**). In that same search for "life insurance," we see that some listings have organic site links to terms like "Life Insurance Basics" and "Life Insurance Checklist." These links are Google's best guess at the next step a user might want to take.

People also ask	⋮
What is the average life insurance cost per month?	⌄
What are the 3 types of life insurance?	⌄
Is it worth paying for life insurance?	⌄
What is the best life insurance policy?	⌄
	Feedback

FIG 2.4: Google's "People also ask" box shows the most commonly asked questions around the search query's subject matter.

"People also ask" boxes

The "People also ask" box is a SERP element that tries to answer some of the most common questions users have around the search query (**FIG 2.4**). As you interact with the box, it automatically adds more related questions to the list. To investigate search intent here, interact with each question and see what kind of content is provided in the answers. Take note of any additional questions that populate further.

Local packs

A *local pack* is a SERP feature that shows local business listings related to your query, usually accompanied by a map (**FIG 2.5**). When Google inserts a local pack into the search result, you can confidently surmise that there's some form of visit-in-person intent behind the search. In our life insurance example, we can infer that—along with seeing intent around insurance definitions and product overviews—people might find life insurance daunting to navigate on their own, and would like to reach out to someone locally who can help them make the best purchase decision.

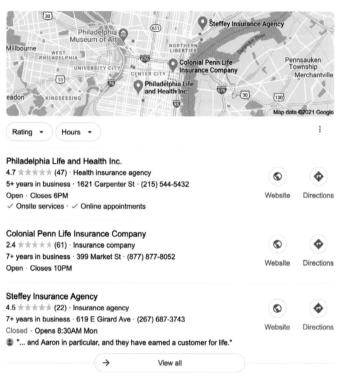

FIG 2.5: A local pack appears when Google determines that the searcher wants to visit a brick-and-mortar location—in this case, an insurance provider's office.

---

https://www.policygenius.com › life-insurance ⋮

Life Insurance: Policies & Free Online Quotes | Policygenius

Life insurance provides a tax-free lump sum of money to your loved ones, called a death benefit, after your death. Explore our policies and save up to 40%.

Who needs a life insurance... · Life insurance rates · How do I buy life insurance?

People also search for	✕
life insurance quotes no medical exam	life insurance companies
life insurance quotes over 50	life insurance rates
term life insurance	best life insurance quotes

FIG 2.6: Google's "People also search for" box appears when a user returns to the search results after visiting a link.

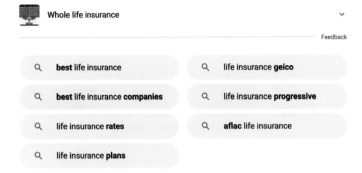

Related searches ⋮

Whole life insurance ⌄

Feedback

Q **best** life insurance

Q **best** life insurance **companies**

Q life insurance **rates**

Q life insurance **plans**

Q life insurance **geico**

Q life insurance **progressive**

Q **aflac** life insurance

FIG 2.7: The "Related searches" box at the bottom of every SERP may show you topics that haven't appeared in basic blue links.

"People also search for" and "Related searches" boxes

If you return to the SERP after visiting a link, you'll see a new SERP element appear: the handy "People also search for" list. These are additional search queries that are similar to the original, but might differ based on your search history or the initial search listing you clicked on. However, from Google's perspective, the return visit to the results page means you didn't find what you were looking for at the visited link, so it will suggest alternate paths to satisfy search intent.

Take note of any new topics addressed in these links: they may help you satisfy more areas of intent (if they apply to you, of course). For example, the linked phrases in the "People also search for" box in our life insurance search suggest a new subcategory that we haven't seen yet: life insurance for seniors (**FIG 2.6**). If you were a life insurance company redesigning your site, you might want to create a page dedicated to this topic, or to address questions around life insurance for seniors in your general page content.

The "Related searches" box that sits at the very bottom of every search result page attempts to provide the same supplemental information and serves the same purpose in your investigation (**FIG 2.7**).

FIG 2.8: A knowledge panel for a search on "disability insurance" includes a definition and information about waiting periods, benefits, costs, and reasons for purchase.

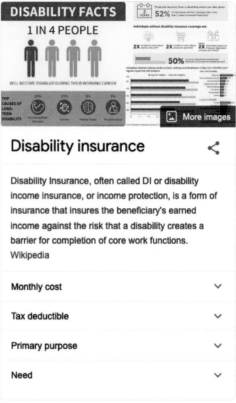

Knowledge panels

Knowledge panels appear in the top portion of some SERPs, and reflect answers supplied by Google's Knowledge Graph, which can be seen as the output of all the connections Google has made between the data it has found on the web. The panels may contain images, Wikipedia definitions, dates, statistics, cultural notes, or other data Google deems relevant to the search query (**FIG 2.8**). Knowledge panels are a very telling source of search intent. Google doesn't insert this feature into all of its results, so when they do, take heed!

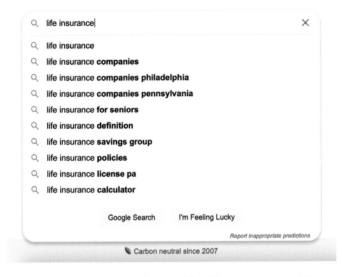

FIG 2.9: Google's predictive search is a useful tool for uncovering search intent.

Incidentally, there's nothing you can do to ensure that a particular search query or keyword will get a knowledge panel. Only Google controls when a knowledge panel will appear, and whether an organization, brand, or person has enough authority and relevance to merit one.

Predictive search dropdown

Lastly, scan for ideas in Google autocomplete (FIG 2.9). As you input search terms and phrases that are relevant to your product, service, or subject matter, Google's predictive dropdown feature can tip you off regarding common queries, local relevance, and trending topics. (Be sure to use your browser's private browsing mode so your own search history doesn't impact the search results you see.)

Themes of intent

If you've ever conducted user interviews, you know that talking to just a couple of people isn't quite enough research to uncover overarching themes. Themes only become apparent after looking at your insights in aggregate.

Studying the SERP for search intent works sort of the same way. It's important to review the entire SERP and all of the features shown for each of your root terms. Yes, it's natural to see some repetition in SERP elements here—the related searches and search phrases that crop up again and again are *themes of intent*. Google is showing you the top forms of search intent for your root term. The themes you see most often are typically the most important, and may even correlate to higher search volume.

SERP features vary by query; you won't see the same features with every search, and while some of the features will show the same intent, others will present new ideas. Scan everything to make sure you don't miss any important forms of intent.

To continue with our life insurance example, if you framed your themes of intent as potential content topics, your list might look something like this:

- Life insurance basics: definitions, how it works, types of insurance
- How to choose the right plan
- Comparison chart between types
- Validation: reviews, awards, best-of lists
- Life insurance checklist
- Average cost per month
- Average cost by age group
- Life insurance for seniors
- Get a quote online
- Cash value of life insurance plans
- Life insurance calculator (how much coverage do I need)

You can address this search intent in many ways—from improving existing web content and creating new pages to making navigation changes and adding new features and functionality. We'll talk more about how you can address search intent in Chapter 4. As with all search intent, the organic search visibility wins don't come from addressing just the biggest themes you see; they come from addressing *all* of them (as long as they're appropriate for your organization).

ANALYZING THE CURRENT SEARCH STATE

Analyzing the SERP is a research method based on how you'd *like* to be found in search engines. But you can also learn a lot about search intent by researching *how people find your site now*, and what they look for once they get there, by looking at the data in Google Search Console and your onsite search.

Google Search Console

The words and phrases people use to find your site now can give you insights into which of your current users' tasks are most common, which problems they're looking to solve, which topics are generating traffic (and which ones aren't), and which pages or page types are driving that traffic.

The only true source of this data is Google Search Console. It's a free tool that provides insights into organic search performance, as well as information about how Google is indexing your site. One of the tool's biggest strengths is the depth it provides in keyword-level reporting: it tells you the literal search queries people are using to find your site. While you aren't able to see which keywords are leading to conversions, the tool does report on which keywords lead to the most *impressions*, or how many times your site appears in search results for each keyword, as well as the traffic those keywords generate.

Only your organization has access to this data—it's only accessible to a verified site owner. If you haven't set up an account for your site or verified the site owner yet, follow the instructions from Google support (http://bkaprt.com/seo38/02-05). Once you're verified, you can analyze the keyword data by logging into Google Search Console, navigating to the Search

FIG 2.10: Once you have access to Google Search Console, run a search performance report (accessible in the left-hand navigation). Select a date range in the top bar, then QUERIES in the lower pane. Search Console also offers *Page* and *Query* filtering functionality if you're looking to narrow down your focus to a specific page, a subset of URLs with a common URL structure, or searches that include or exclude specific words or phrases. Query filtering is commonly used to filter the difference between branded and non-branded searches.

results section, and exporting the data as a spreadsheet. For example, in a dataset from the Google Search Console account of a company that provides supplementary insurance, we see queries like "how does short term disability work" and "how much does short term disability pay" (**FIG 2.10**).

The queries shown in this example (from a product page for short-term disability insurance) indicate a clear theme of intent: *how does disability insurance work?* In a sense, this theme is about practical details like: *How will I get paid? How much can I expect to receive? How long will it take to get my benefits?*

In the world of supplementary insurance, transparency and practical information about how various plans work are often avoided because of policy variation and perceived legal constraints. Even if you don't work in insurance, the pressure to remove web content details that actually benefit users might be familiar to you. But identifying significant search intent around sensitive information in your keyword or onsite search data can help build a compelling case to create more transparency in site content. Giving users the content they truly need to succeed—that's a major win.

Whatever themes of intent you uncover, analyzing your Google Search Console data can lead to unique insights that your competitors don't have access to—data that's unique to your site, especially when it comes to brand-related searches.

Onsite searches

Studying your onsite search logs (in Google Analytics or wherever you store that information) can reveal how people currently search within your website. Some users prefer onsite search functionality to navigate websites, while others only use it as a last resort to find what's seemingly unfindable. Taking the time to understand what information is most commonly requested or hard to find within your site structure is extremely valuable for spotting unmet themes of intent. A high volume of similar search queries in your onsite search data can indicate either that content isn't clearly labeled in the navigation or that the website doesn't address the subject matter at all.

ANALYZING KEYWORD DATA

Google collects raw keyword and search volume data from users conducting search queries, which SEO platforms like Ahrefs, Moz, and Semrush then add to their own databases. These platforms offer many tools for finding insights in keyword data.

Before you dive into keyword research, set the scope of your analysis. It's scalable and can be made to adapt to the complexity of your project. Here are some common dependencies to consider:

- **Popularity of the subject matter:** The popularity of your research topic is usually directly proportional to the amount of available data and number of relevant keywords. The more popular your subject matter, the more search data you'll have to sift through and assess.
- **Project size:** The complexity and scope of your project can drastically change the scale of your keyword research. A full site redesign requiring research on multiple products or services will entail significantly more work than a project focusing on a specific section or page.
- **Business value:** The significance of the project to your organization can also be a major driver of scope. Research on an organization's most critical product line, or on a topic that is paramount to the future of the organization's success, will matter more to the business than research on an average article page. When there's more at stake, you can expect to spend more time on detailed research.

Assess the context for your project and use it to define the scope and depth of your keyword research.

Select your tool

There are a lot of great keyword tools to choose from. At the time of writing, Semrush, Ahrefs, and Moz are your best options because they offer the deepest set of keyword data and provide a more accurate estimate of search volume using *clickstream data* (detailed logs of how users navigate websites during a task or session). This data is collected only from users who opt into sharing it with browsers, which then share that data with keyword research tools.

All three tools offer similar pricing, but there are slight differences in their available features and which dataset they use. Tools do evolve, though, so it's wise to do a little research on your own before making a final decision. Whatever you end up choosing, don't choose Google's Keyword Planner for this type of research; because it's made for paid search, it's not very transparent.

Generate root terms

To start, you'll need to formalize your list of *root terms,* the basic words and phrases most commonly used to describe your products, services, or topics of information. For example, if you're selling life insurance, some root terms might be "supplementary insurance," "universal life insurance," "whole life insurance," or "life insurance."

To get a good list of root terms going, jot down the most common terms for your products, services, or topics, as well as any terms you want your site to rank for. Focus on nouns and verbs. If your list feels light, or if you have a product or service that's less well known or hard to describe, you can look for terms in a few other areas:

- Review any available user research that highlights why people come to your site, what they hope to find, what problem they want to solve, and what words they use to describe your topic.
- Talk to paid-search folks about which keywords convert best for them—those terms are likely to resonate with users.
- Check out chat logs, contact forms, and customer service emails to pick up on what language users choose to describe things.

Make sure you're exploring as many angles as possible to generate a comprehensive list of terms. Remember, the output of your research will only be as good as your input.

Keep in mind that your final list will likely have dozens of root terms. If your organization has a very extensive line of products or information, like a big-box store or major publisher, your root terms may be in the hundreds—in which case, prioritize your research around key products, services, or topics, and then chip away at them iteratively.

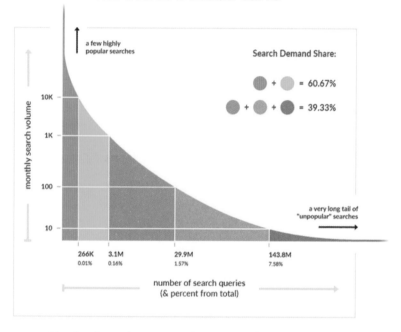

The Search Demand Curve

a few highly popular searches

a very long tail of "unpopular" searches

Search Demand Share:

● + ○ = 60.67%

● + ○ + ● = 39.33%

monthly search volume

10K
1K
100
10

| 266K | 3.1M | 29.9M | 143.8M |
| 0.01% | 0.16% | 1.57% | 7.58% |

number of search queries
(& percent from total)

FIG 2.11: Most Google searches on a given day are so specific and uniquely worded that the search volume for exact phrases used is quite low. These keywords make up the long tail of the search demand graph. In aggregate, these long-tail searches far outnumber highly popular searches (http://bkaprt.com/seo38/02-06).

Look to the long tail

Once you've got your list of root terms, enter them into your keyword data tool. The data compiled for each root term shows *long-tail keywords*—more specific searches tailored precisely to what users are looking for (**FIG 2.11**).

Although long-tail keywords aren't as popular or broad as high-level root terms, they make up a substantial percentage of searches around any given topic and reveal the search intent around that topic. (Don't make the mistake of thinking that *long tail* means longer keywords! Keywords can be any length; *long tail* refers to their place in the extremely long tail of a search demand curve.)

Keyword	Volume
life insurance	246,000
term life insurance	49,500
whole life insurance	49,500
life insurance companies	33,100
life insurance policy	33,100
life insurance quotes	33,100
senior life insurance	22,200
best life insurance companies	18,100
best life insurance	14,800
term vs whole life insurance	12,100
universal life insurance	12,100
what is term life insurance	12,100
types of life insurance	9,900
cash value life insurance	8,100
is life insurance taxable	8,100
term life insurance quotes	8,100
life insurance rates	8,100
what is life insurance	8,100
what is whole life insurance	8,100
how does life insurance work	6,600

FIG 2.12: We've exported the keyword data around the root term "life insurance" into a spreadsheet, along with each keyword's corresponding monthly search volume. A quick scan reveals several search intent themes: costs and quotes (highlighted in yellow), types of life insurance plans (in blue), and definitional information (in pink).

For example, if you plug the root term "life insurance" into your keyword tool, you will see long-tail keyword searches like:

- "whole life insurance quotes"
- "what is term life insurance"
- "how much does life insurance cost"
- "types of life insurance"

Every long-tail keyword on the list of results has the root term "life insurance" in it. In order to identify useful themes of search intent, you'll need to look at the additional words around the root term that make up each long-tail search phrase. For example, nouns like "quotes," "cost," and "rates" demonstrate an emerging theme around cost information. Phrases like "definition," "what is," and "meaning" show a theme of understanding insurance terminology. And words like "universal," "whole," "term," and "types" show a theme of types of insurance plans (**FIG 2.12**).

PRIORITIZING RESULTS

Put your exported keyword data into a spreadsheet so you can work with it more easily. It makes sense to pull groups of related root terms out into their own spreadsheet tabs. For example, terms like "life insurance," "disability insurance," and "accident insurance" are all types of insurance products, so you could group them in the same tab to quickly spot themes across products.

In each tab, you'll need several columns, starting with one for the keywords, and another for the corresponding search volume. You'll also want several other columns for categorizing your keywords thematically, which will help you understand search intent priorities.

Categorizing the keywords

For each keyword, identify and assign a theme in one of the columns. You use data filters to save time in this process. For example, if you use the filtering tool to show only keywords that contain "rates," you can assign the first entry with the theme of "Costs" and copy it all the way down—instantly categorizing thousands of keywords at once.

The further you advance through this process, the more theme categories you'll create. When appropriate, look for opportunities to connect related categories into a larger theme (this is where multiple columns come in handy). For instance, in our life insurance keyword data, you can see search queries for insurance for seniors, children and families, survivors of serious illnesses, veterans, and others (**FIG 2.13**). By creating a higher-level theme called "For types of people," you can categorize five or six themes into one. The more specific themes can be included in another column as *subthemes*, which you can use to segment your data further at the end of the process.

High Level Topic	Theme	Sub Theme 1	Sub Theme 2	Keyword	Search Volume
Product - Accident	For types of people	Children		accident insurance for child	20
Product - Accident	For types of people	Students		k-12 student accident insurance	30
Product - Life insurance	For types of people	Survivors		life insurance for cancer survivors	170
Product - Life insurance	For types of people	Survivors		cancer survivor life insurance	70
Product - Life insurance	For types of people	Survivors		life insurance cancer survivor	20
Product - Life insurance	For types of people	Survivors		can cancer patients get life insurance	20
Product - Life insurance	For types of people	Survivors		life insurance after a heart attack	50
Product - Short term disability	For types of people	Self employed		short term disability insurance for self employed	70
Product - Short term disability	For types of people	Children		short term disability childbirth	30
Product - Short term disability	For types of people	Children		short term disability child support	30
Product - Short term disability	For types of people	Family		is short term disability paid family leave	20
Product - Long term disability	For types of people	Self employed		long term disability insurance for self employed	30
Product - Long term disability	For types of people	Mental illness		long term disability insurance mental illness	20
Supplemental, voluntary Health	For types of people	Seniors		supplemental health insurance for seniors	170
Supplemental, voluntary Health	For types of people	Seniors		best supplemental health insurance for seniors	50
Supplemental, voluntary Health	For types of people	Seniors		supplemental health insurance for seniors with medicare	30
Supplemental, voluntary Health	For types of people	Veterans		supplemental health insurance for veterans	20
Supplemental, voluntary Health	For types of people	Seniors		supplemental medical insurance for seniors	40
Product - Life insurance	For types of people	Children		life insurance plans for child	30
Product - Life insurance	For types of people	Family		life insurance plans for family	30
Product - Life insurance	For types of people	Seniors		life insurance plans for seniors	20
Product - Life insurance	For types of people	Veterans		veterans life insurance death benefits	50

FIG 2.13: Categorize your keywords by theme, looking for opportunities to identify both higher-level topics and more detailed subthemes.

Summarizing the search volume

This is the best part. No, really! You've gathered keywords and created a detailed categorization of themes—now you finally get to see which themes of intent are most important to users.

Pivot tables are handy for summing up search volume and breaking it down by theme of intent. In your pivot table settings, choose the themes (or subthemes) you'd like to analyze and display the sum of search volume. Now, instead of confronting an endless list of keywords, or a flood of search volume numbers, you can see how many times real people search for your identified themes in aggregate (**FIG 2.14**).

You can also use pivot table data to create charts, which can tell a more user-focused and visually captivating story about search volume to internal stakeholders. Pie charts, in particular, humanize the search data. They're like a magic trick that turns search volume into percentages of *people* who care about each theme of intent (**FIG 2.15**).

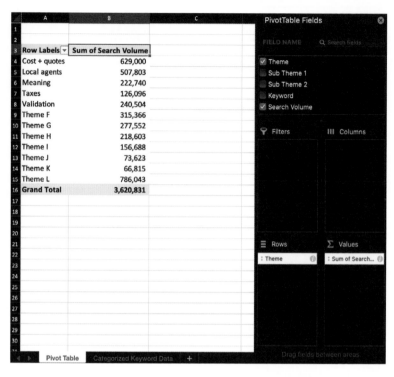

FIG 2.14: Pivot tables (like this example in Microsoft Excel) can tally up search volume for each of the themes you've identified.

Sharing search intent research with stakeholders

Now that you know more about what your audience expects from your site, you need folks in your organization to seriously consider addressing that search intent. You want your data to effect real change in your site's content and design.

Some people will be excited about seizing organic search opportunities, and others might not be. Perhaps they worry that search intent data is really just a way to make them write and design "for robots." But the way you present your data, and the language you use to talk about search intent, can make a big difference! Here are a few tips:

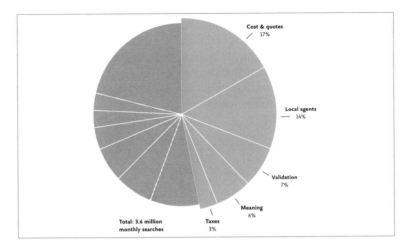

FIG 2.15: Pie charts shift the focus from pure numbers to the actual percentage of people searching for different themes. For example, instead of saying, "The search volume for cost and quotes was 629,000," now you can say, "Seventeen percent of people are looking for information on cost and quotes."

- **Avoid jargon and focus on users.** Instead of saying "search volume," say "the number of people who care about this" or "the number of times people are looking for this information." Reiterate that you and your colleagues are solving problems for real users, not just for search engines.
- **Use pie charts and percentages instead of bar charts and quantities.** Pie charts demonstrate how each category of search intent is a piece of the whole—it helps keep the conversation on the larger user experience. Bar charts frame the data differently, emphasizing the popularity of individual categories over the relationship to the overall scope. This can encourage cherry-picking, leading people to fixate on satisfying only the most popular areas while ignoring others that are just as essential to the successful completion of the user journey, despite their lower search volume.

- **Present search intent research alongside other user research.** Whenever possible, present search volume research along with interviews, user journey maps, or survey results so that stakeholders can get a holistic picture of the user experience and see the search journey as part of the overall customer journey.

WHEN SEARCH INTENT RESEARCH ISN'T A GOOD FIT

It's rare, but not impossible, that you'll run across a research topic with little or no search data surrounding it. Maybe it's an ultraspecific niche that's relatively unknown, or a newly trending topic. Maybe you spot a few people searching around your root phrase, but there isn't enough long-tail data to reveal any discernable themes of intent. Whatever the case may be, when there's no search data, there's no search intent to reveal, and that's that.

But before throwing in the towel, take more time to explore. It's extremely rare to find subject matter that no one has searched around. It's more likely that you haven't identified the search angle people are really using, or the topic is so new that the data around it isn't showing up in standard search tools yet.

Check out Google Trends to investigate the popularity of emerging topics. Consult with teammates running paid-search campaigns for your organization. Look to terminology your competitors are using in page titles and headlines on the homepage and key product pages. And don't forget: talking to real customers is always extremely helpful.

So far, we've discussed research for SEO in terms of search intent. But SEO research isn't limited to search intent analysis, nor is search behavior limited to marketing—it's intertwined with the user experience. In the next chapter, we'll explore ways to add a search perspective to the user research you already do.

3
SEO AND THE RESEARCH YOU ALREADY DO

“ *You can optimize everything and still fail, because you have to optimize for the right things. That's where reflection and qualitative approaches come in. By asking why, we can see the opportunity for something better beyond the bounds of the current best.*
—ERIKA HALL, *JUST ENOUGH RESEARCH*

WHETHER YOU'RE A DESIGNER, writer, developer, or marketer, you are a person with a goal: you want to make sure your website is findable. You want the digital experience you're creating to actually meet people's search intent—to give them what they're looking for.

Including an SEO lens in the research process is one of the most important steps you can take toward achieving your goal. As we've seen, Google is a database of human psychology. Once you start leveraging this database to account for user search behavior, you won't be able to stop seeing how search ties into everything. You'll naturally find ways to use search data to build a clearer picture of your audience and their needs, and notice gaps in the experience where you're not meeting search intent.

A caveat: we're going to discuss flexible strategies for adding a search lens to common user research tactics, not how to approach research practices as a whole. If you're just getting started with research and aren't yet familiar with the methods we discuss here, we highly recommend checking out Erika Hall's invaluable *Just Enough Research*. It'll give you a solid foundation around how to approach research more holistically.

While you could certainly add a search lens to nearly any form of research you're already doing, we recommend integrating search considerations into these four key activities:

- **Stakeholder analysis.** Asking the right questions of senior leadership or any other folks who are critically invested (but not always directly involved) in your project will help you uncover any organizational reasons behind current SEO challenges, determine goals and opportunities for SEO, and shine a light on culture or process problems that impede search visibility. This is critical for SEO success, so we're going to spend a good deal of time on this activity.
- **User interviews.** There's no substitute for hearing what real users say about how and why they use your site. Unearthing users' search habits can provide surprising and helpful insights. Depending on how complex or specialized your subject matter is, you may want to talk to users prior to search intent analysis to begin building your list of root keywords. If you've already analyzed keywords, interviews can help you fill in the blanks around the data and better understand how search fits into the user's journey.
- **Content audits.** If you're embarking on a redesign or doing any kind of iterative design work, taking a closer look at the content you already have is especially important for SEO. You can use search-relevant metrics to help shape your audit criteria, and then use the results to uncover gaps in search intent.
- **Competitive analysis.** With a little sleuthing and help from a few inexpensive competitive-research tools, you can see how your site stacks up, SEO-wise, against competitors. This can help you pinpoint gaps in performance, see how links

and authority play into your site's visibility, and learn what topics your competitors are (and aren't) covering.

In this chapter, we'll walk through strategies for conducting research activities with SEO in mind.

SEO AND STAKEHOLDER INTERVIEWS

We once worked on a project with a company that had moved its entire blog off their main site and onto a subdomain, not realizing the negative impact such a move would have on search visibility. Microsites can't leverage the authority and links of the main domain, so they generally don't perform as well in organic search.

Many internal constraints led up to the microsite decision. The marketing department wanted the blog to use plain language, but the legal department imposed restrictions on terminology used on the main site. The UX department wanted the blog to have a different look and feel, but the IT department lacked the developer resources to build out new page templates and navigation. Faced with these roadblocks, the blog team decided a microsite was their only option.

We talked to team leads and higher-up stakeholders to dig deeper and learn more. It turned out that leadership didn't realize that the legal team was being so inflexible, or that the IT department was so underresourced. They *definitely* didn't know that building content on a microsite would have negative implications for SEO—and once they did know, they were determined to remove the roadblocks that had kept the content off the main site in the first place. That's real progress that would never have happened if we hadn't asked about search considerations in our stakeholder interviews.

Choose people to interview

As in any stakeholder interview process, the first step is to identify whom you need to talk to. Who are your SEO stakeholders? The biggest challenge there is that most people won't realize that they are, in fact, SEO stakeholders. They might not see the connection between their goals and the role search plays in reaching those goals. Asking the right questions can help them see those connections.

Start by making a list of all of your project stakeholders, noting the roles they play, as well as their actual names and titles. Then categorize your list to help identify gaps and overlaps. We use the seven stakeholder categories created by content strategist Meghan Casey (http://bkaprt.com/seo38/03-01):

- **Sponsors**, like VPs or directors of digital or omnichannel, get the recognition or take the fall for organic search visibility. There's often only one sponsor, but not always. Sponsors are usually responsible for the strategy and success of the company website and typically determine the role SEO will play in achieving that success.
- **Financial decision-makers**, like VPs of marketing who lead a company redesign, decide whether SEO and search intent analysis get funded. Again, there's usually only one of these, but there could be more. They're ultimately responsible for funding SEO efforts, but might not understand SEO's value or anticipate the investment it requires.
- **Strategic decision-makers**, like UX directors whose performance is partially measured on the website's alignment to user goals, have a problem that SEO can or should solve. They will likely be vocal about findability, and may be concerned that "optimizing for machines" could impede usability.
- **Champions** are people you can count on to evangelize the importance of search and its role in design and content. A champion could be anyone influential and well-regarded in your organization who understands the value of human-centered SEO (and is willing to help you socialize research and win support for SEO integration).
- **Derailers** don't have official veto power, but they typically feel that SEO is a threat to their goals. Depending on their influence, derailers can (intentionally or unintentionally) stop a user-centered search strategy in its tracks. They're often outside the obvious pool of project stakeholders but are impacted by the project outcomes, like creative direc-

tors who think "off-brand keywords" will undermine voice and tone.

- **Influencers** have opinions and insights worth considering, but they don't have veto power. They could be subject-matter experts, product managers, or even customer-service managers who can help you understand how people search for your content and the topics you should be ranking for.
- **Implementers** are responsible for putting search strategy into action and bringing SEO to life. They often make content and design decisions that have a direct impact on search visibility. An implementer could be someone a lot like you—a web writer, designer, search professional, or developer.

While having stakeholders in these different roles will go a long way toward making your endeavor successful, it's also important to ensure you have balanced departmental representation involved in the website strategy, from marketing to technology to paid search.

Questions to ask

Once your list of stakeholders includes the right mix of people to move your search-friendly agenda forward, it's time to add an SEO lens to your interview questions. The questions we ask aren't set in stone, but we typically start with an interview script that will uncover anything that could have a major impact on our work and help us neutralize politics, understand priorities, set expectations, and identify opportunities.

In addition to asking people for their name and title—and any other research questions you might have—here are some basic questions to draw out SEO-relevant insights.

To learn about expectations, ask:

- What role does organic search play in our strategy?
- What does a successful SEO strategy look like to you?
- What changes in organic search rankings would you like to see in a redesign? Why?

- What do you wish you knew about our users and the way they search?
- Where does organic search fit into the redesign process?
- Who's responsible for organic search outcomes?
  To identify opportunities, ask:
- How does paid search fit into our strategy right now? (Sometimes overreliance on paid search can stem from an issue with organic SEO and signal that there is an opportunity to get more of that traffic for free.)
- For paid search:
- What search terms topics do you typically bid on?
- What types of keywords typically convert best?
- What's the monthly budget? (Monthly budgets can help you understand where your organization is spending the most money. You may want to prioritize SEO efforts there first, in terms of business priorities and cost savings.)
- What's the return on investment? (This can help you understand underperforming areas that might need better alignment with search intent.)
- Do we have separate digital properties or websites? How many? (SEO challenges can emerge when similar content competes against itself or lacks the domain authority necessary to achieve high rankings.)
- What roles do these other sites play? How did we decide on this domain strategy?
  To understand priorities, ask:
- How does your team define success?
- What is the role of the website in achieving that success?
- What factors impact your team's raises, promotions, hires, and resourcing?
- How will we measure success for the website?
- What areas of the website are most important to you and your team? Why?
- What areas of the website are most important to your customers? Why?
- What user segments are a priority for you right now?
- What products or services are a priority for you right now?
  To neutralize politics, ask:
- Is there anyone else we should be talking to about this?

- If you've tried to implement SEO in the past unsuccessfully, where did it go wrong?
- Are you aware of any negative perceptions or concerns around SEO? What would it take to change that perspective or resolve those concerns?

What to watch out for

Inevitably in your interviews, you'll come across workflow red flags, conflicting priorities, or unhealthy expectations that could derail your SEO efforts. Make note of those and plan out action items to mitigate them.

Workflow risks and concerns

As you talk to managers and implementers, you will very likely discover that content, design, and development teams have no idea how intertwined their work really is with SEO outcomes. You might discover that people are wary of SEO in general, and thus actively avoid serious efforts to include it. Even if people are open to it, you might see challenges in workflow, timing, or coordination that you'll need to get ahead of.

Instead of avoiding troublemakers, invite any potential derailers (especially influential ones) to the initial strategy and project-planning work sessions. (If that's too much involvement, at least share your project goals and plans with them. Invite them to discuss where their work might intersect, any key areas where they need to provide feedback, or other ways they could participate.) You want them to take as much ownership of the process as they can, so they feel heard and invested in success. If you get stuck, lean on sponsors and champions to help soften attitudes or change perspectives to set the stage for process and workflow changes when necessary.

Competing priorities

"Doing SEO" might involve conducting search intent research, making changes to site navigation, writing new content, optimizing meta descriptions and titles, and taking on a whole range of technical tasks that we aren't even covering in this book. Because it's usually not feasible to do everything at once, focus your SEO efforts on high-priority areas of your site—but note that this only works if those areas have already been clearly established and prioritized. If stakeholders are unable to agree upon which areas of the site are most important in terms of earning organic visibility, it will be difficult to focus your SEO efforts.

High-priority areas of the site are usually those tied to real business outcomes like generating leads, selling a product or service, or even just drumming up awareness around specific information. Business outcomes are *not* site-performance metrics, like increasing traffic or reducing the bounce rate. If you hear metrics like that stated as business goals during interviews, dig deeper to get to the desired business outcomes those metrics are meant to drive, and *then* map them to areas of the website that most clearly support those outcomes.

After your interviews, you might find that different people have different ideas about which areas of the site are most important in terms of SEO. To clarify competing priorities, hold a working session with key stakeholders:

1. Display a list of all of the different areas of the site with organic search concerns, based on what you heard during the interviews. Ask if anything's missing that should be added to the list.
2. Have participants rank those areas of the site in order from most to least important in terms of organic visibility. If you're working with a smaller group (no more than eight people), you can simply have folks talk through the prioritization. When working with larger groups, dot voting can be a good way to assess priorities democratically: give participants a limited number of dot stickers to vote on which areas of the site are the most important to them. How many stickers you give each participant will depend on how many priority areas you need to narrow your list down to. Have everyone vote quietly, without discussion or lobbying. In the end, tally up the dots. Areas of the site with a higher concentration of dots are higher in priority.

3. Assess the outcomes of this working session against the search data and insights from your search intent analysis.
4. Create a rolling optimization task list that aligns SEO efforts to high-priority areas of the site. Then use that to determine what pages or sections you're going to focus on first.

Unrealistic expectations

Knowing what people expect SEO to do can help you communicate appropriate expectations early on. Here are some of the most common holdups we see:

- **Getting hung up on the visibility of a single keyword or specific search phrase.** If you do organic search right, there should be myriad ways someone can find your content, and many different points of entry too. Don't let the idea of The One Perfect Keyword create tunnel vision—you want to be looking at a bigger, more nuanced picture of visibility across many different search terms in a category.
- **Expecting specific SERP features.** As you may recall from Chapter 2, SERP features are nontraditional organic search listings like knowledge panels or "People also ask" boxes. You can optimize for these and hope for the best, but there's never any way to make sure Google will include your website in their structured search result components.
- **Expecting content on microsites and subdomains to gain significant search visibility.** Like we discussed earlier, content on microsites and subdomains can't benefit from the main site's *link authority*—the quality and quantity of links a page has that give it more value to search engines. Search engines treat microsites as entirely separate; regardless of any connection to a parent site, they'll have to be indexed from scratch. With subdomains, it's not impossible for them to earn visibility, but it is typically challenging.
- **Expecting traffic for products or services that nobody is actually searching for.** If there's no search demand for the information your content is providing, you can't reasonably expect that if you optimize that content, the traffic will come.

In such cases, a public relations campaign or paid advertising would be better tools than organic search.

To address unrealistic expectations, it's helpful to demonstrate how your site is doing in organic search right now. This could happen by way of an informal presentation where you teach stakeholders how modern search works and highlight any current organic search performance issues. You can use this opportunity to dispel SEO myths, clarify misconceptions, and set more realistic shared expectations. See Chapter 6 for more ideas about sharing search considerations with your team.

SEO AND USER INTERVIEWS

We once worked with a hotel client that was redesigning its website. The client wanted to use SEO to encourage people to book rooms directly on its site, rather than on third-party travel aggregators (like Travelocity). They saw organic traffic as a zero-sum game: users either went directly to their site (good for the client) or booked on third-party sites (not good for the client).

But as we conducted user interviews, we learned that both the hotel website and the third-party sites were an important part of the user journey. Most users we talked to started their hotel-booking process on a third-party travel site to get an idea of their options and costs. But once they identified a hotel that seemed like a fit, they almost always visited the hotel site directly to see more details about the rooms or to look at pictures.

This meant we didn't have to try to outrank the third-party travel sites for the most popular keyword terms (which is nearly impossible to do anyway). Instead, we focused on improving the user booking journey on the site itself by optimizing the local visitors-guide content and map results to show up earlier, improving key messaging on the homepage, and elevating direct booking deals in other areas of the site.

Talking to real users about the reasons behind their searches helped us fill in the gaps from the search intent analysis and make smarter design decisions that aligned with what people actually wanted to know about the hotel. Search intent analysis and user interviews complement each other quite well, because together they provide the whole picture of search behavior. The data tells you *what* people are searching for; the interviews tell you *why* they are searching for it—and the combination can be pretty empowering.

You might be thinking, "Hey, now...user interviews are about way more than just understanding how and why people search!" And you'd be absolutely right. Keep on doing what you do in user interviews—just add in a few SEO-related questions to learn about search behavior, too.

Depending on your specific project needs, you might choose to conduct user interviews before researching search intent, or vice versa. If you research search intent first, you can use interviews as a way to close knowledge gaps around the data. But if you're doing research for an industry that is technical, niche, or just very unfamiliar, doing the interviews with real users first can help break down complex search paths and expose insider lingo and potential root terms and keywords to research.

Selecting people to interview

The nice thing about adding a search lens to user interviews is you don't have to add any new groups of people or user types to the list—everyone uses search! You're simply adding questions to your interview guide that will evoke search insights from the people you've already planned to talk to.

Of course, different user segments have different goals and priorities, and your organization might have different goals or content segmented by audience type, too. Because of this, it's possible you'll need to tailor your search-focused questions to your user types.

Questions to ask

The list of questions we ask users varies from project to project. The exact questions you ask will be determined by the context of your product, service, or subject matter. You'll also want to consider whether the search has a transactional, informational, navigational, or visit-in-person context, like we discussed in Chapter 2.

Here are some sample search-focused questions we typically ask—you can modify them to meet your needs.

To learn about how people discover websites like yours, ask:

- Have you ever searched for information around this product/service/topic online?
- Were you able to find the information you were looking for?
- How did you decide if the information was trustworthy or not?

To learn what their search journey looks like, ask:

- Tell me about the last time you looked for a product/service/topic like this online. How did you begin looking for information? What did you do next? (Keep in mind that they might not always start with a web search. Their search journey could begin with talking to someone in person, following a link from Twitter or Reddit, or doing a Google search. The point here is to find out and uncover the journey.)
- How did you decide what to do? Will you walk me through the steps leading up to your purchase/decision/action?
- How did you research your decision online? (This is a slightly different angle to pull out missing steps in the journey if they haven't covered it fully.)

To learn how search plays into the experience of current customers or users, ask:

- Can you tell me about the last time you used our company's website?
- Did you visit the site directly or start with a Google search (or another search engine)? If so, why?
- Were you able to find the information you were looking for?

Even if the questions you're asking aren't specifically designed to draw out search insights, you can still get search-relevant insights by listening to users tell you about their context or challenges. You're listening for how search plays into their experience, as well as the terminology and language they use to describe your topic.

Identify search behaviors and goals

As you go through your interview notes or call recordings, notice things users said that could impact your site's search strategy, content, or design. In particular, be on the lookout for how users might be expressing search behaviors and search goals.

Search behaviors are actions or decisions that users make when performing a search. These behaviors can help you understand how and where search fits into the user journey, and which pages or areas of the site you should prioritize for search visibility. In user interviews, search behaviors sound something like this:

- "We always pick our hotel based on the activities we're doing on the trip. So I plan out our trip itinerary, and then search for hotels that are close to what we're doing on that leg of the trip."
- "I usually click the links with good ratings. I don't really notice the search results without ratings."
- "I started off looking at 'best-of' articles or lists when I was researching our last vacation. When I found somewhere that felt like a fit, I'd check out Travelocity to see what hotels would cost us, and then dig a little deeper on ones that stood out."

Search goals are users' desired outcomes for a search—the tasks they're trying to accomplish. Search goals help you understand which pages need to exist and what information they need to deliver. In user interviews, search goals sound like this:

- "When I'm prepping for a trip, I'm looking for local mountain biking trail maps above all else. It's frustrating when that information is only available in a PDF and I can't tell if it's what I need until I skim over the whole document."

- "I'm pregnant and want to take a vacation that's easy and relaxing, so I'm looking for the best babymoon destinations."
- "Charlie, our dog, always goes on road trips with us. Pet-friendly rooms are our top priority. I like to look at the room layout and get a feel for the property too, like how far we'll have to walk him to go potty or get a run in."

Try to capture the remarks as near to verbatim as possible. People's exact words and phrases are useful for keyword research, copywriting, and stakeholder presentations. Don't lose that valuable language behind summaries and paraphrases.

Turn themes into recommendations

Once you've identified search behaviors and goals, you need to translate them into actionable next steps for content, design, and code.

Start by grouping search behaviors and goals into thematic categories. You'll start to notice which search needs are the most common or crucial—or which search needs you had assumed were relevant but were actually mentioned by very few users. Categorizing will also help you prioritize your recommendations and action items.

For example, during user interviews for our hotel client, we heard some folks mention specific search terms like "family-friendly hotels." Others identified search behaviors like seeking out user-generated photos of hotel rooms to gauge whether the layout would be spacious enough to share with family members. Other users emphasized the importance of swimming pools and play areas when traveling with young children, and how having a mini-fridge and private bathroom vanity area made sharing rooms with family easier. When we looked at those search behaviors and search goals together, the theme became clear: users wanted family-friendly hotel rooms.

Themes made it easier to see what design and content changes needed to happen to better support the search experience—and ultimately create a better user experience, too. To help users find the family-friendly rooms on the hotel site, we made some recommendations to our client:

- Create a page for family-friendly rooms, and make sure the page is highly visible in the site navigation.
- Describe family-friendly amenities (like the playground and swimming pool) in both the meta description *and* introductory copy for the page, even if they're already included in the list of amenities present on all room pages.
- Include mobile-friendly pictures of family-friendly suites along with diagrams of room layouts, and make sure the alt text for each image includes the terms "family-friendly hotel rooms" and "kid-friendly hotel" where relevant.
- Use keywords like "family-friendly hotel" and "group suites" in the page's headings (h1 and h2 tags) where relevant.

As this small sample of recommendations demonstrates, SEO can touch anything from the site navigation to the copywriting to the imagery. When making your own search recommendations for a project, consider every element of the digital experience: What user needs did you hear? What questions did people ask? What does your website need to do in order to solve their problems? It will take a combination of content, design, IA, functionality, markup, and marketing to pull everything off.

SEO AND COMPETITIVE ANALYSIS

You probably already know the mix of brands in your market basket, but what about your search competition? When someone searches for your product, service, or information, they will *always* have choices. You should know what those choices are—whom you're competing against, directly and indirectly, for search visibility. With a bit of manual sleuthing and a little help from inexpensive tools, you can better understand the competitive landscape in terms of search performance.

Here's what you'll scope out in your competitive analysis:

- **SERPs and your competition.** Who shows up—and how do they show up—in Google search results when you do a search for your main products, services, or information?

	Visibility, %	Avg. position	Traffic	SERP features	Positions Improved	Declined	#1–3
☑ ▼	8.57 +0.14	23.70 ▼ 2.53	90.8K −2K	76 +16	▲ 60	▼ 109	68 −2
☑ ▼	0.03 −0.01	23.60 ▲ 2.93	319 −92	2 −1	▲ 21	▼ 79	3 −2
☑ ▼	0.35 −0.03	27.04 ▲ 0.88	3.7K +249	14 +4	▲ 168	▼ 63	15 +4
☑	2.59 +1.06	28.74 ▼ 1.38	27.4K +10.6K	38 +10	▲ 120	▼ 85	51 +8
☑ ▼	0.28	38.46 ▼ 0.64	2.9K −129	13 +8	▲ 46	▼ 57	6
☑	0.98 +0.11	27.35 ▼ 0.71	10.3K +723	17 −12	▲ 80	▼ 139	34 −2

FIG 3.1: This is what the Rank Tracker panel in Ahref's Domain Analytics tool looks like. Reference the Competitor Overview section to get a sense of how you rank compared to your competitors.

- **Traffic and authority.** How does your domain stack up against competitors in terms of traffic from organic search? Is your site at an advantage or a disadvantage from a link and authority perspective?
- **Gaps in content topics covered.** What content topics are your competitors getting visibility for that you don't cover?

SERPs and your competition

If you've gone through the search intent research process outlined in Chapter 2, you'll already have a list of root terms that represent the core information, products, or services on your site. Search for these terms in private mode (you don't want to be logged into your browser) to get a cursory list of organizations your site competes with in search.

Make a list of all of the organizations you see in the first two pages of search results. Then look at what they offer, the problem they're solving, and the experience their site provides to narrow the list down to your three to five closest competitors.

Add these top search competitors to your existing list of competitors, and use a tool like Ahrefs or Semrush to get a sense of comparative rankings (**FIG 3.1**).

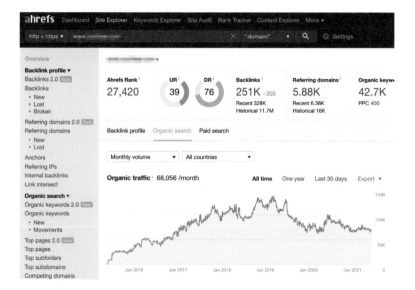

FIG 3.2: In addition to keyword research, tools like Ahrefs can also provide estimated organic search traffic insights for any website.

Estimated traffic

Many of the same keyword research tools we used in Chapter 2, such as Ahrefs and Semrush, can provide valuable competitive insights (**FIG 3.2**). These tools have access to an extensive set of keyword data, monthly search volume associated with each query, and insight on which sites rank for each query—which means they can provide an *estimate* of monthly organic search traffic for a site.

These estimates vary in accuracy, especially if your organization is regional or outside the United States. To gauge how accurate these estimates might be, first compare what each tool says about your site to what you actually know—you'll probably see some inconsistencies. Then, when you look at the data for your competitors' sites, keep that same margin of error in mind.

Link authority

As we've discussed, a high volume of inbound links from authoritative websites can help improve your site's rank in search results, so it's smart to know how you and your competitors measure up. Using your keyword research tool, look at the number of:

- **Referring domains.** *Referring domains* are sites that link to your site. A high number of referring domains typically means more authority. The authority of the linking sites matters, too: the more authority a referring domain has, the more authority it grants your site.
- **Backlinks.** As you may recall, *backlinks* are the number of actual links coming from those referring domains. As with referring domains, the more backlinks coming from authoritative sites, the better.

Looking into your competitors' referring domains and backlinks can help you gauge how their authority might factor into SERP rankings. For example, if a competitor with comparatively subpar content is outranking your site and excelling in their referring domains and backlinks, you might deduce that those factors contribute to their competitive edge in search results. How did a weak website earn such quality backlinks? Maybe their site is just older and more established, and therefore more sites link to it. Maybe their brand is so well known that Google believes they should appear in search results, so they can get away with satisfying less search intent than you. Whatever the reason, if your site lacks referring domains and backlinks by comparison, it might be a good time to chat with your PR folks about developing a solid organic link-building strategy.

On the other hand, if you have the link advantage but aren't getting more visibility than your competitor, this may mean your content doesn't satisfy search intent as well. Your next step should be to look for potential gaps in your content.

FIG 3.3: King Arthur has multiple "special diet" categories accessible from their main navigation. Beyond being helpful for users, this page contains "paleo" in the URL and links to their gluten-free, low-carb, and paleo products—which helps the company earn visibility in all of those categories.

Gaps in content coverage

Look at the information architecture and content of your competitors' websites to understand their topics. Identify the sections, subsections, and individual pages within each part of the site; don't worry about keywords, but try to notice the coverage and subject matter. Which content topics do they address that you don't?

Take, for example, baking supply companies King Arthur Flour and Arrowhead Mills. Although they both sell grain-free flours that could be used in gluten-free, low-carb, or paleo diets, only King Arthur uses those terms in their navigation (**FIG 3.3**). Arrowhead Mills positions the same products as "gluten-free," without using terms like "low-carb" or "paleo" (**FIG 3.4**). For reference, "paleo flour" has ten times the search volume of "grain-free flour"—shouldn't products that fit that description rank for that search term?

King Arthur also includes recipes and blog posts with words like "keto" and "paleo" (**FIG 3.5**), but no high-level category pages to group those recipes together. Two dedicated URLs with links to all their paleo and keto recipes, respectively, would improve their search visibility for those topics even more.

FIG 3.4: Arrowhead Mills carries flour that could be considered paleo- or low-carb-friendly, but because they don't have any product category pages or menu items with those labels, they are likely missing out on search visibility.

FIG 3.5: Multiple recipes, products, and blog posts appear when searching for "keto" on the King Arthur website, but a dedicated keto topic page to connect this content would be even better for search visibility.

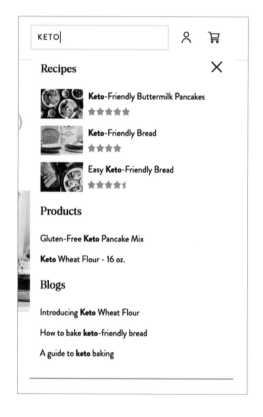

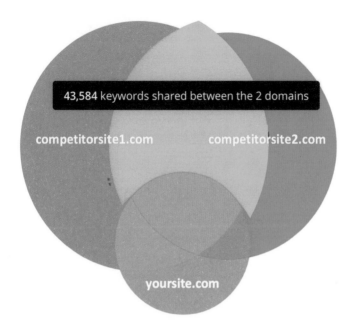

FIG 3.6: SpyFu's Kombat tool shows how many keywords overlap in the content for your site and competitors' sites, as well as the keywords they share that you don't (in this case, over forty thousand keywords).

Tool features like Content Gap (in Ahrefs) and Kombat (in SpyFu) can also help identify content gaps. These can show which keywords you share with your competitors and which you don't (**FIG 3.6**), which can highlight potential opportunities for your site. You can also see the keywords ranked in order from highest search volume to lowest. Think of these keywords as potential content topics rather than searches. When a site has visibility for a keyword that you don't, they likely have content on a topic you don't cover on your site.

You can also use some tools, like Ahrefs, to understand which pages, sections, or subdomains on your competitors' sites generate the most organic search traffic. To access this information, run a Top Pages report and study the list of Top Keywords (**FIG 3.7**). Do you see any topics that you haven't

#	Traffic	Value	Keywords	RD	Page URL	Top keyword	Its volume	Pos.
1	57,767 2%	$50,249	29,483	11,102	...com/	...	111,000	2
2	32,582 1%	$16,990	82	41	...com/lash-sensational-sky-high-mascara? productid=pimprod2020260	maybelline sky high mascara	65,000	1
3	19,316 <1%	$6,323	2,204	124	...com/james-charles-palette?productid=pimprod2001848	james charles	459,000	6
4	15,647 <1%	$6,656	279	90	...com/infallible-fresh-wear-24hr-foundation? productid=pimprod2002481	loreal infallible foundation	37,000	1
5	14,933 <1%	$6,687	363	70	...com/brand/body-shop	the body shop	127,000	5
6	14,003 <1%	$5,832	202	44	...com/grandelash-md-lash-enhancing-serum? productid=pimprod2003445	grandelash serum	15,000	1
7	13,284 <1%	$2,159	455	173	...com/aha-30-bha-2-peeling-solution?productid=pim-prod2007102	the ordinary peeling solution	46,000	3
8	13,177 <1%	$6,341	581	140	...com/skincare-oil?productid=xlslmpprod1800041	bio oil	79,000	3
9	13,007 <1%	$11,454	441	25	...com/black-opium-eau-de-parfum?productid=xlslmp-prod12951153	black opium parfum femme	8,300	1

FIG 3.7: With Ahrefs Top Pages, you can generate a report from your competitor's site that shows you their top-performing pages, what keywords those pages are getting visibility for, and an estimate of the traffic those pages are driving to their site.

already identified? This report is handy because it doesn't just identify content gaps for you; it identifies the most popular content on your competitors' sites, the content their users find the most helpful and actively search for. Taking this extra step is a good way to help prioritize which content gaps you should tackle first.

Analyzing the competitive landscape is an important part of content research and a prudent precursor to content auditing. Sure, you can audit the content you've got now against SEO best practices and your own set of criteria, but if you're trying to rank in search results, you also have to audit your content against the sites you'll compete with for search visibility. You'll identify content gaps, learn more about why domains are ranking (and possibly outranking you), and hopefully find opportunities to meet search intent in more useful and relevant ways.

SEO AND CONTENT AUDITS

If you're working with content you already have (as opposed to planning for all new content), content audits are essential, especially for your search strategy. Although it's common to see separate audits for UX, content, and SEO, that can lead to conflicting recommendations or duplicated work. You can avoid that by considering these three intertwined disciplines all in one audit.

Ideally, someone with a search background can pair up with a content strategist or UX designer to cocreate the audit criteria and tackle the work together. That way, the SEO specialist can ensure the audit covers the technical aspects of SEO. (If you want to learn more about what technical aspects to consider, check out Chapter 5.)

But even if you're not a seasoned search professional, or this kind of collaboration isn't possible on your team, you should still audit content to ensure it meets basic SEO best practices. It's not just a matter of checking for on-page optimization and keyword targeting—it's about using search metrics to home in on valuable content that should be included in your site audit, making sure that content satisfies search intent, and uncovering where search optimization can make the biggest impact.

Set up your inventory

At its most basic, a content inventory looks like a spreadsheet listing all of the URLs on your site, often including individual files and PDFs. This is the most thorough way to capture and assess all available content.

In addition to a column for URLs—and any other columns you use in your content or UX audits—you'll want to add columns for each metric you'll use to analyze search performance. Start with some metrics that are available in your site's analytics platform:

- **Landing-page sessions.** This is the aggregate traffic from pages where users first enter your site. Filter this metric for organic search to measure how much organic traffic any given page brings into your site.

- **Page views.** A *page view* represents a single instance of a page being seen by a visitor. If a user reloads the page, or navigates elsewhere and then returns, a second page view is recorded. Make sure any pages on your site with high page views get included in the audit—those are highly visible (and important to search) pages! You should also audit any pages that your business considers important but that have disproportionally low page views.
- **Bounce rate.** There are a lot of misconceptions about how a bounce is defined. But we'll tell you here plainly—a *bounce* is a single-page visit to your site, with no visits to any other pages in the site in the same session. For example, if a user reads an article on your site but doesn't visit other pages, that's considered a bounce—even if they hang out on the page for twenty minutes! A high bounce rate isn't necessarily bad; in fact, it can be a good thing if the page was designed to give the user all of the information they need right there. However, if your pages were designed to lead people deeper into your site, a high bounce rate likely indicates a problem. When someone visits a page from the SERP and doesn't find what they're looking for, they typically return to the search engine to continue their search. Google considers this *pogo-sticking*, which can negatively impact your rankings.
- **Time on site.** *Time on site* is the average amount of time a user typically spends on a page. It's important to note that if a user only visits one page (a single-page session), Google Analytics can't track how much time is spent on that page. Too little time on site (except on pages designed specifically to direct visitors elsewhere) may indicate that users can't find what they're looking for.
- **Conversions.** A *conversion* occurs any time a visitor to your site completes a desired action (e.g., watches a video, downloads a file, makes a purchase, etc.). If you've set up conversion tracking in your analytics package, you'll want to grab that data for your audit, ideally including any macro or micro conversions you're tracking.

We also recommend including some metrics and data that can be found in other tools:

- **Linking root domain count.** *Linking root domain count* refers to the number of unique domains linking to a specific page on your site. As we mentioned earlier, the more sites that link to a URL, the more potential that page has to rank in search, so these pages play an important role in your current visibility. This metric is available in any SEO tool, like Moz or Ahrefs. Look particularly at pages with high linking root domain count in your audit to make sure the content is shipshape. Ensure these pages aren't accidently removed in a redesign (without accounting for the positive impact they have on your search visibility).
- **Page titles.** Each page in your site has a `title` tag, a short description that tells search engines what the page is about; the title appears at the top of the browser window and in SERPs. Titles should be no longer than sixty characters; longer titles are truncated and could look weird or, worse, misleading in SERP results. The website crawling tool Screaming Frog SEO Spider can show you all the page titles for your site.
- **Meta descriptions.** This data is also available in Screaming Frog SEO Spider. A *meta description* is a tag in a page's HTML that shows a summary (up to 156 characters) of a page's content in SERPs. Meta descriptions are extremely important to the search experience, and they deserve as much love and care as the copy on your homepage. They're literally the first thing a user sees in the SERPs, and often determine whether or not they'll click through to your site at all.

Now, you could export all of this data from each platform separately, but if you want to save time, Screaming Frog SEO Spider can actually collect all of it for you. Their platform has API access to nearly every other SEO tool and analytics platform out there, including Google Analytics, Google Search Console, Page Speed Insights, Ahrefs, and Moz. So instead of running five separate reports manually, you can collect several different platforms' worth of data from a single source.

Choose your pages

In addition to getting a complete list of everything living on your site, the main reason to create an inventory is to determine what content you'll *actually* audit. Unless you have a website that has fewer than a hundred pages, there's a good chance you'll only audit a portion of your site's content, such as a particular section, a set of key pages, a specific content type, or a sampling of subsections.

If you want to audit a sample of the overall site experience, choose pages that represent a range of content types, page templates, and site sections. Be sure to include:

- Your homepage
- Key product and service pages
- Pages that are important to your brand or responsible for communicating key messages
- Pages you know are important to users
- Pages with time- or date-sensitive content
- Landing pages that lead to the most conversions
- Pages with high page views
- Pages with high landing-page sessions
- Pages with high landing-page sessions *and* high bounce rates (a sign that they might need improvement with forward paths into the site and internal linking)
- Pages with high linking root domain count
- Pages that are underperforming (i.e., pages that are essential to your business or that you believe should be popular, but with page views or conversions that suggest otherwise)

Once you've narrowed down your inventory, you should have a more manageable spreadsheet of URLs to audit. What's more, you can be confident that your audit won't accidentally overlook pages on your site that are important to users, pages that are playing an important role in your site's organic search visibility, or underperforming pages that need attention.

Audit your content

Now you're ready to take a closer look at your content's search visibility factors—to actually audit. You're auditing your selected content in order to answer the following questions:

- **Does the content include on-page optimization?** Check each URL for the on-page elements that optimize visibility and drive traffic, such as: headings and body content with appropriate keywords; links to pages with related subject matter elsewhere on the site; appropriate authority and trust signals (like author bios and credentials); semantically relevant anchor text for links; and accurate image alt text.
- **Does the content satisfy search intent?** If you've done the research outlined in Chapter 2, you should have some idea of what the major categories (and subcategories) of search intent are for each of your products, services, or topics. Add a column to your spreadsheet for search intent, assign the relevant theme of intent to each URL, and then review each page to see how well its content, features, and functionality satisfy the intent.
- **Is the content optimized for SERP display?** Here, you're auditing to make sure each page has the necessary elements to be as eye-catching, appealing, and helpful as possible in search results. Look at the `title` tag and meta description, check for applicable Schema.org markup, and consider content formatting and presentation.

If all of this sounds like an exact science, please remember *it isn't*. While there are a few "yes" or "no" boxes to tick, most of this is gut-based and tied to your own assessment skill level. We'll walk you through best practices for optimizing many of these elements in Chapter 4.

When it comes to the nuts and bolts of the audit, adding a single column to your spreadsheet for *every single* SEO element you're looking at would be overwhelming and unwieldy. Instead, you can make aggregate evaluation easier by adding columns for each of the three categories we just mentioned: on-page optimization, search intent, and SERP display.

Stick to whatever grading scale you're using for the rest of your audit work, or feel free to use ours: we use a scale of 1-3, where 1 is the worst score (none of the category criteria are met for a specific element) and 3 is the best score (all of the criteria are met). We sometimes use half-points if we need more nuanced scores. Use a notes column to cite exactly what's weak or missing. You can also download an audit template with the criteria we use (http://bkaprt.com/seo38/03-02) (**FIG 3.8**).

Whatever grading system you use, remember that it takes time and experience to understand which items in your audit will make the most impact for organic search, and how to weigh that impact against the effort it will take to implement those improvements. Your goal is to include an assessment of your content's SEO strengths and weaknesses in search *alongside* your general content audit in order to avoid duplicative or even conflicting recommendations. This will help you identify opportunities for improvement in meeting users' search intent holistically through content, features, functionality, and other aspects of user experience.

Incorporate data into decision-making

Your newly acquired SEO data can help validate (or push back on) content, design, and business decisions for your project. Without that data, you could end up removing pages that are important to users—satisfying multiple forms of search intent, answering critical questions, and providing helpful context about complex services. If such pages are deemed irrelevant to the project's strategy, instead of simply deleting them, you can *reframe* them to support your strategy while retaining their search value.

Adding a search lens to your content audits will not only make you incredibly familiar with the ins and outs of your site's search elements, but will also give you a sense of what's working well, what needs improvement, and which patterns point to sitewide issues rather than one-page problems.

As you know by now, SEO is about so much more than key-words and headlines. It's about using all of the tools we have to communicate meaning and context to search engines while making information easier for humans to find. In addition to

	A	B	C	D	E	F
1	Unique ID	URL (Current)	URL (Future)	Audience	WED (Write, Edit, Delete)	Landing Page Sessions
2						
3						
4						
5						
6						
7						
8						
9						
10						
11						
12						
13						
14						
15						

FIG 3.8: This snapshot of our audit document shows a few of the criteria columns we use to capture data about web content.

serving as a holistic starting point for improving content, SEO, and UX, your audit findings will help you set performance and success metrics for your search strategy moving forward.

RESEARCH WRAP-UP

Adding a search lens to stakeholder interviews, user interviews, content audits, and competitive analysis is useful for making design decisions that lead to successful search outcomes. But it's not the only way you can go about incorporating SEO into your research practice. Once you get comfortable with how SEO works and grok the basic metrics used to measure search behavior, you'll find new ways to add SEO considerations to whatever forms of user research your team already uses. And most important, you'll start to see that optimizing for search is truly tied to creating a better user experience overall.

In the next chapter, we'll discuss practical ways to use what you've learned in research to make search-friendly design decisions that make humans happy, too.

4 SEO IN DESIGN AND CONTENT

❝ *I think we should stop thinking of it as Search Engine Optimised and more that it is human optimised content. I mean, that's the whole point of SEO, isn't it? To get to the human. It seems like a silly distinction to make but I find the way we talk about what we are doing influences how we are doing it.*

—SARAH WINTERS, "SEARCH ENGINE OPTIMISATION (SEO) AND CONTENT" http://bkaprt.com/seo38/04-01)

YOU NEVER KNOW WHEN a seemingly ordinary project will turn into an opportunity to do truly meaningful work. That's what happened for us while working on a site redesign for a health insurance provider. The client had embarked on a redesign to reorganize their health plans—along with their site navigation—solely by level of coverage (that is, by bronze, silver, and gold plans, with high, medium, and low deductibles). It was a pretty straightforward approach.

But after we conducted search intent research to understand how people actually look for health insurance information, it became clear that health insurance is about *much* more than deductibles and copays. Buying health insurance is really buying peace of mind, and peace of mind is personal.

That story was told by search data. When people search for health insurance, they research plans that fit their specific situation or medical needs. Search categories like health insurance *for seniors*, health insurance *for mental and behavioral care*, health insurance *for pregnancy*, and many others began to emerge. In fact, the total search volume from people who wanted to learn more about health insurance for *their* specific circumstances was just as significant as the number of people searching for costs and quotes.

This data helped guide many of our design decisions—from the navigational structure of the site (where we organized health plans by specific circumstances and types of care shown in the search data) to the core content, features, and functionality of the pages themselves.

Now that you've gathered search-specific insights for your project, it's time to use them to guide the content and design decisions ahead. Beyond using search data to design better experiences, search engine intent must be accounted for at key points in the content and design process for effective SEO:

- user journey mapping
- information architecture and navigation
- content planning
- content production

Let's unpack how SEO overlaps with each of these key points in the process.

USER JOURNEY MAPPING

User journey maps are a model of the experience your audience has with your website. If you use them in your current design practice, you know that, first and foremost, these maps try to capture what users are doing, thinking, and feeling at each point along the way.

You can add search behaviors and search intent data to your user journey maps to get a better sense of how search plays into the online bits of the journey during each phase. Not only does this make keyword data more accessible to a larger stakeholder audience, but it also helps you identify steps and mindsets in the user journey that might previously have gone unaccounted for:

- **Steps.** Search steps commonly appear as a user searching in Google before they reach your website, or returning to Google to compare information. Make sure the way you capture these steps in the journey reflects the user's intention, too. Were they trying to compare? Research? Validate a decision?
- **Mindsets.** Other key components of any good user journey map are the thoughts, questions, and information needs users have during each phase of the journey. Keyword data is excellent for identifying this stuff: long-tail keywords are often made up of questions, thoughts, and information needs.

The search steps and mindsets you identify in your research will often correspond with different phases of your user journey maps, but where they land will depend entirely on the phases you've defined. For example, imagine a user journey map for an athletic shoe retailer with four major linear phases:

- **Discover:** the reason for seeking out the product, service, or company—typically "I have a need or problem" searches. You're looking for keywords and phrases that capture the reason behind the need that drives interaction with your site in the first place. These searches usually express informational search intent and might look like: "feet hurt while running," "running routines," or "how to get in shape."
- **Research:** the steps users take to define their needs and explore their options. In this phase, you're looking for "I need to decide among options" searches. Here, the user has defined their need—in this case, "I need new running shoes"—and is looking to compare, validate, or get more specific information. Searches in this phase might include: "best running shoes 2020," "best running shoes for flat feet," "Nike running shoe reviews," or "New Balance vs. Nike running shoes."

- **Buy:** the purchase or transaction. Searches in this phase are made up of "I need to find a thing I want to buy" searches. The keywords and phrases tend to be specific: "Nike Epic React Flyknit 2 SE black size 9.5," "gray running shoes for women," or "running shoes next day shipping."
- **Support:** the post-purchase relationship with the user. Support-related searches are all about "I need help with what I bought." They sound like this: "Zappos customer service," "Nike return policy," or "best way to clean Nike Flyknit shoes."

While these phases make sense for an online ecommerce journey, your phases might look very different depending on your site's context and purpose. No matter what phases make up your user journey, they will likely include a mix of offline and online steps. Keyword data can help you better define all the steps and unpack the user's mindset around them (**FIG 4.1**).

If you really want to get fancy, visualize the search opportunity of each phase by mapping themes of search intent to the user journey. If you've done keyword analysis like we outlined in Chapter 2, take your big keyword spreadsheet with correlating search volume and add a new column to map the search terms back to the user journey phase they relate to (**FIG 4.2**). This will also give you an idea of search volume for each phase. Voilà—you've mapped search volume to the journey (**FIG 4.3**)!

The magic of this step is that once you know which phases of the journey correlate to the highest search volume, you can compare them to the content on your site to identify gaps. For example, perhaps you discover much of the search opportunity around running shoes happens during the research phase. If you don't have content on your site that satisfies this search intent, you won't be able to help users find the information they're looking for. Consequently, you won't be able to win organic search visibility in that phase of the user journey, either.

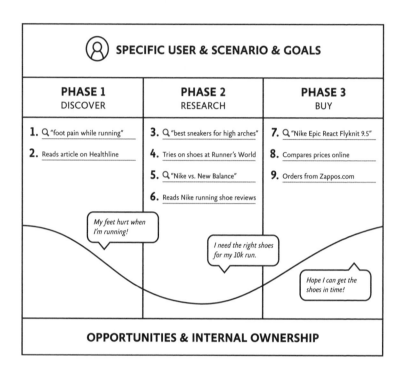

FIG 4.1: We've pulled actual keyword data from our search intent analysis and overlaid it directly onto the steps of this user journey map, alongside offline actions. The user mindset conversation bubble in Phase 1 was drawn from search data, too. You could make this even more detailed if you quantified the search volume of each keyword you add to the steps.

	A	B	C	D	E	F
1	Theme	Sub Theme 1	Sub Theme 2	Journey Phase	Keyword	Search Volume
2	Validation	Best		Research	best running shoes for women	60,500
3	Validation	Best		Research	best nike running shoes	18,100
4	Validation	Best		Research	best trail running shoes	14,800
5	Manufacturer	Nike		Support	Nike return policy	12,100
6	Brand	Return Policy		Support	zappos return policy	9,900
7	Color	White		Buy	white nike running shoes	8,100
8	Condition	Flat feet		Research	best running shoes for flat feet	8,100
9	Condition	Flat feet		Research	running shoes for flat feet	6,600
10	Condition	Plantar Fasciitis		Research	best running shoes for plantar fasciitis	6,600
11	Gender	Women	Color	Buy	white nike running shoes womens	5,400
12	Validation	Best		Research	best running shoes 2020	5,400
13	Validation	Best		Research	best adidas running shoes	5,400
14	Validation	Best		Research	best asics running shoes	5,400
15	Brand	Customer Service		Support	zappos customer service	4,400
16	Condition	Arches		Research	best running shoes for high arches	4,400
17	Exercise	Get in shape		Discover	how to get in shape	4,400
18	Validation	Best		Research	best long distance running shoes	4,400
19	Validation	Best		Research	best running shoes for overpronation	3,600
20	Validation	Best		Research	best stability running shoes	3,600
21	Validation	Best		Research	best cushioned running shoes	3,600
22	Condition	Plantar Fasciitis		Research	running shoes for plantar fasciitis	2,900
23	Exercise	Get in shape	How long	Discover	how long does it take to get in shape	2,900
24	Diagnose	Pain		Discover	top of foot pain running	2,400
25	Diagnose	Pain		Discover	foot pain from running	2,400
26	Exercise	Get in shape	Back	Discover	how to get back in shape	2,400
27	Condition	Bad Knees		Research	best running shoes for bad knees	1,900
28	Gender	Women	Color	Buy	all black running shoes womens	1,600
29	Exercise	Get in shape	Women	Discover	get in shape for women	1,300
30	Gender	Women	Manufacturer	Buy	nike flyknit running shoes womens	1,300

FIG 4.2: We've added a new column (Journey Phase) to our keyword spreadsheet to correlate search data with phases in the user journey. This isn't an exact science; we're taking our best guess at which phases the keywords naturally match, which helps us quantify search opportunities.

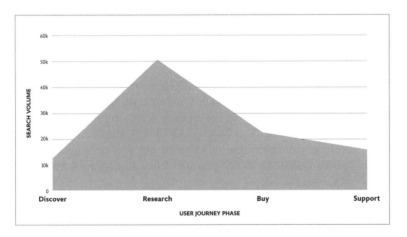

FIG 4.3: Identify potential content gaps by comparing phases with high search volume to existing site content and the traffic in those related site areas.

INFORMATION ARCHITECTURE

Information architecture (IA), the practice of "organizing, structuring, and labeling content in an effective and sustainable way," is the foundation of good usability (http://bkaprt.com/seo38/04-02). The goal of IA is to make sure users can find information easily and complete the tasks they came to do. Coincidently, this sounds a lot like the goal of SEO.

Essentially, IA underpins your entire content ecosystem: what will be on your site, where it will live, and how each page will be labeled. Not only is IA valuable for search visibility, but what something is named in the navigation also communicates its semantic relevance to Google.

When it comes to SEO and IA, there are a few things you must consider as you go about your business.

To page or not to page

If you don't have clearly organized and labeled content around something, it will not rank. Creating a dedicated page with helpful, relevant, and unique content on a given topic will boost that topic's search visibility and ranking—and it will serve your audience. If the page doesn't serve your user, it might not be worth creating.

Creating pages purely for SEO is never a good idea. As Sarah Winters of Content Design London says, "If you think about SEO purely being for the human searching for information then you wouldn't get 'SEO pages'" (http://bkaprt.com/seo38/04-01). As you determine whether or not you need a new page, some questions to ask yourself from an organic search perspective include:

- **Is there a product or service that needs to be represented?** There should always be a page dedicated to each individual product or your organization's core offering.
- **Is the information critical?** Think of content like a return policy, legal notice, or code of conduct—it might be brief, but because of its essential nature, it needs to be easily found.

- **Is there enough to say about the topic?** Topics that are relevant to your business goals and user needs will naturally generate content. If you don't have much to say about something, that suggests you don't need to create a dedicated page.
- **Is there too much to say?** When you have a lot to say about a topic, breaking your content into shorter subpages might better align with ways people search for that information. It makes the information easier to find in organic search, and easier to navigate and digest onsite, too.

Ultimately, the pages you create are for real people who are trying to find your subject matter. The content must always be designed to meet their needs.

Follow your users' leads

While working on a site redesign for one of the oldest and most respected speakers' agencies in the US, we learned that most users looked for a specific type of speaker for their event, one they had already determined would be a good fit. The search data revealed, not surprisingly, that the two most popular ways people searched for speakers were by topic—"conference speakers on healthcare and medicine," for example—and by type—"women keynote speakers"—or a combination of both. But we also learned that leadership wanted to use the top navigation to showcase their "about us" page, which focused on their reputation, exclusive speakers, news, and curated programming ideas. This buried the speaker categorization and search filters several pages deep in the site's structure. They weren't considering what users wanted in the nav; they focused on what *they* wanted. This is how it had always been; this was what the agency's leadership felt the most comfortable with.

But leaving the topical speaker search out of the main navigation would have been a missed opportunity from an organic search perspective, and it would have made it harder for people to complete their primary task.

Thankfully, the search intent data was compelling enough to change leadership's mind. They ultimately included speakers by

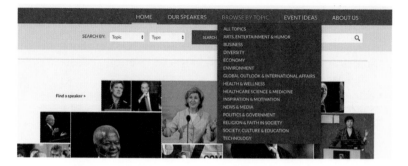

FIG 4.4: The redesigned site addressed the most popular form of search intent (speakers by topic) in the main navigation, and the second-most popular form (speakers by type) in the omnipresent speaker filter.

topic in the main navigation and made sure the ability to filter speakers by topic and type was an omnipresent search option (**FIG 4.4**). Furthermore, we were able to identify exactly which speaker topics and types were most popular in terms of search volume and made sure those were listed first in the navigation and filtering options.

In her book *Everyday Information Architecture*, Lisa Maria Marquis says, "Look for the words (especially the verbs!) that people use when interacting with your site or product, then mirror their language back to them." For this site redesign, the words people used in their searches not only informed category labels; they also implied a larger task that needed representation in the navigation to fully satisfy search intent.

Whether you organize information using an exact system (chronologically, alphabetically, or geographically) or subjectively (by topics and tasks), you can study search intent data and listen for clues in user interviews to see how people search, and then use this data to make better information architecture decisions for your site.

Use content hierarchies to show relationships

The way content is categorized and subcategorized can help pages improve in search results. This is true for high-level top-

TOPICS	
The search rankings for top-level categories...	**CODE**
	Application Development 36
	Browsers 108
...are directly impacted by the links and content from pages in the subcategories.	CSS 158
	HTML 165
	JavaScript 116
	The Server Side 45
	CONTENT
	Community 51
	Content Strategy 62
	Writing 51
	DESIGN
	Brand Identity 20
	Graphic Design 80
	Layout & Grids 71
	Mobile/Multidevice 37
	Responsive Design 35
	Typography & Web Fonts 47

FIG 4.5: The links and content from subcategory pages will directly impact the search rankings of the high-level category.

ics that correlate to more general search terms, as well as for specific subtopics that correlate to long-tail search terms. The key here is that *both* types of pages need to link to each other (**FIG 4.5**). High-level category pages must contain links to their subcategories, and pages within the subcategories should link back to the parent category.

This tells search engines that the pages are related in terms of subject matter. Pages with high link authority pass equity along to linked pages. This means that where content is subcategorized directly impacts the ranking ability of its parent category. Although the purpose of categorizing content is to make it easier for people to find what they're looking for, don't forget about the signals you're sending to search engines. How you subcategorize content will impact what topics you do or don't gain search visibility for.

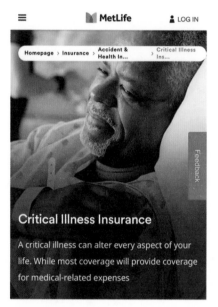

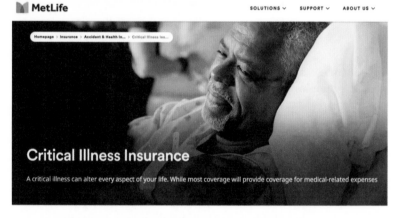

FIG 4.6: To save space on small screens you could remove the homepage link and use truncated breadcrumbs, as MetLife does here.

Breadcrumbs are beneficial

With organic search, any page in your site can be the first place a user lands. Breadcrumbs and navigational highlights help users orient themselves within your website and understand how the page they're on relates to a higher-level category. Beyond the UX benefits, breadcrumbs also serve as an internal linking structure that gives search engines a better understanding of how your pages are contextually related to one another. Google now displays breadcrumbs in search results and uses them to categorize information on the SERP as well.

Harness the benefit of breadcrumbs by making sure they're near the top of the page and visible when the page loads, and at every screen size (not just on desktop). Since Google primarily crawls your site from a mobile perspective, you'll need those breadcrumbs on smaller screen sizes in order to provide clear connections between various categories of content (**FIG 4.6**).

Subdirectories over subdomains (and microsites)

Where content lives impacts not only the user experience, but also search visibility—and link authority plays a role here, too. Link authority consolidates more value (and gains strength) when high-value pages live under one domain rather than being spread over multiple domains or properties.

Getting IA right means considering three things: your users' needs (particularly around understanding and navigating content), your brand strategy, and search intent. We suggest addressing these decisions in that order; you can't force what's best for SEO if it doesn't align with brand strategy and actual user needs.

Alas, many organizations don't take any of these factors into account in their decision-making; they simply do what's easiest for the business, like creating microsites and subdomains. Establishing a separate property is often easier than changing the existing site structure to accommodate new content. However, even when owned by the same organization, microsites and subdomains are viewed by search engines as discrete properties where trust and authority must be built from scratch.

Linking to this off-site property from the main site can help, but it can't perform as well as it would if located in an existing site subdirectory. Creating a subdomain or a microsite isn't always the wrong answer, but consider the costs to organic search and user experience before you make a final decision.

URL structure

The humble URL plays a key role in establishing a first impression for both users and search engines: it helps them understand site structure and get a sense of where they are in your site. URLs that reflect a clear folder or site structure path are the most effective for both user experience and SEO.

A few things to consider when it comes to URLs:

- There should only be one URL for any given page. Avoid multiple URL variations that lead to the same page.
- URLs should start with your domain name, followed by the section name, then the next subsection name, until you reach the subdirectory where the web page is located, appearing as a sequence of segments in hierarchal order separated by slashes. Using a flat URL structure, where the URL doesn't contain any of the directory folder sections, is a missed opportunity for usability and SEO. It also makes it harder to track section performance analytics.
- Aim for clarity and human-readable language. Avoid using dynamic parameters; stick with alphanumeric characters that have semantic meaning (**FIG 4.7**).
- The directory and subdirectory folders should reflect the taxonomy of the site for clarity and consistency. Please note that no matter what you hear about SEO, directory and subdirectory folders are not the place for one-off "keyword" opportunities. If your site taxonomy is semantically relevant, your URLs will be, too.
- When it comes to optimizing the *URL slug* (the part of a URL that identifies the specific page), do try to include the main keywords you're trying to gain visibility for. In terms of length, shorter is better than longer; save space by remov-

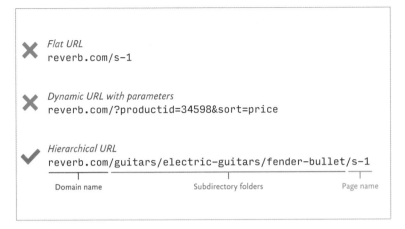

FIG 4.7: A flat URL structure won't do you any findability favors. Neither will dynamically generated URLs that aren't semantically relevant. A hierarchical URL naming structure, on the other hand, tells both users and search engines about the page and its location in the site.

ing conjunctions and prepositions like "to" and "and." Use hyphens between words for readability.

Navigation design

Navigational structures—the main menu, subnavigation, and footer—are the core of what's known as *internal linking structure,* or all the links between your web pages that establish relationships between content and site architecture and spread link equity. Search engines use your website navigation to discover and index new pages.

While your first priority to users should always be ensuring clarity, here are some things to keep in mind when it comes to SEO:

- How you assign visual priority to links helps determine how link authority, or what Google calls PageRank, flows through your site to those pages. In practice, this means links in the footer typically carry less authority than main navigation links, while a bolded text link on your homepage might carry more weight than a link several clicks deep in the main navigation. Make sure pages that need to perform well in organic search are placed prominently and are designed to stand out, can be found easily, or are seen first as a user scans through the page (http://bkaprt.com/seo38/04-03).

- On parent pages containing a list of results, like a blog page with a list of articles or a product category page with a product list, the order in which you list those results shows priority to search engines. When you want pages to rank highly in search, they need to show up on the first page of their parent category pages (not buried somewhere deep within your website).
- Make sure the full functionality of the navigation is available regardless of screen size. Don't truncate the navigation anywhere, even in the footer. Google uses your site performance on mobile devices to determine ranking for *everything*, so it hurts both SEO and user experience to provide a lesser experience for smaller screens. This means that you shouldn't focus on the desktop experience at the expense of how your site loads on mobile devices or its usability on small viewports. A device-agnostic approach will serve you and your users best.
- Google will view pages in your site linked to by other reputable sites as more authoritative. For many sites this is simply the homepage or other pages in the main site navigation. When it makes sense, linking to the most authoritative pages in your site helps distribute authority to the rest of the site. Typically, the farther pages are from the most authoritative pages, or the farther they are from pages linked in the main navigation, the less ranking power they will have.

Done right, navigation design will make it easy for folks to find what they're looking for *and* send crucial signals about the priority of content on the site to search engines. Ultimately, it's important to be intentional about your search priorities and to make design decisions that reflect them.

CONTENT PLANNING

Content strategist Ida Aalen, writing about Are Halland's core-modeling process, said:

> *If you've worked on a website design with a large team or client, chances are good you've spent some time debating (arguing?) with each other about what the homepage should look like, or which department gets to be in the top-level navigation—perhaps forgetting that many of the site's visitors might never even see the homepage if they land there via search. (http://bkaprt.com/seo38/04-04)*

The same can be true when it comes to determining what content, features, and functionality will go on nearly *any* web page, because it means actual people have to agree on priorities. And actual people have a tough time agreeing on much of anything, especially when it comes to competing UX and SEO goals.

Luckily, human-centered SEO and UX goals should never *really* conflict with one another—but if your colleagues aren't in alignment, a collaborative core-modeling exercise can help get all your content and design stakeholders on the same page (pun intended). Inspired by Aalen's recommendations and Halland's core-model template, but adapted to incorporate search considerations, we use this exercise to plan web content for our projects (**FIG 4.8**). You'll need to invite a cross-disciplinary team consisting of content stakeholders and content and design implementers to work together to core-model the page.

While we recommend reading Aalen's full article first, let's walk through the steps we take in the core model exercise:

1. Identify user tasks in search data and balance them with findings from other research.
2. Determine the role search will play in meeting the page's business goals, translating those to search goals.
3. Choose content elements and determine information hierarchy of the page.
4. Consider internal linking structures.

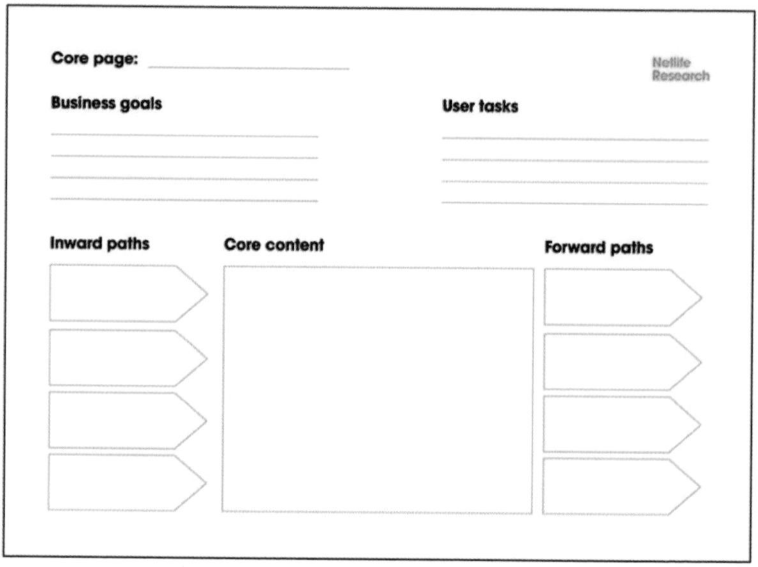

FIG 4.8: Ida Aalen uses this template, designed by Are Halland, to conduct her core-modeling workshops. You can adapt it for planning web page content with a search lens.

Identify user tasks

The first order of business when it comes to planning what content will live on a page is asking, "What is it that people want to get done?" Look to both your search intent analysis and any other relevant user research you have to identify *all* the tasks users are trying to accomplish on the page (not just search-related); then, order them from most important to the user to least important.

For example, imagine you're planning content for a page on pregnancy and childbirth on a health insurance website. After reviewing search intent analysis data, you might make notes around the themes of intent like:

- *"breast pump covered through insurance"—2k searches per month*

- *"best health insurance for pregnancy"—1k searches per month*
- *"health insurance for pregnancy no waiting period"—1k searches per month*

Reimagine the search terms as user tasks by restating them with an active verb, like this:

THEME OF INTENT		USER TASK
"breast pump covered by insurance"		**Learn** which plans cover breast pumps
"best health insurance for pregnancy"	becomes	**Read** reviews from expecting parents and see ratings for our health plan
"health insurance for pregnancy no waiting period"		**See** coverage and plan waiting-period details

Using search queries to identify user tasks and their correlating search volume to estimate priority helps ensure search intent influences content and design as early on as possible. However, as you may remember from our discussion of long-tail keyword data in Chapter 2, even the most popular keywords on a specific topic are no match for the search volume of long-tail keywords related to that topic. So, while the keyword volume for "breast pump through insurance" only amounted to two thousand searches per month, in aggregate, all long-tail searches with this intent might add up to something much more substantial, like fifteen thousand. This is why search volume for individual search phrases can be misleading. It's a good idea to scan your full list of keyword data around a theme of intent and get a sense for which themes have greater volume, or, better yet, sum up the search volume for each theme of intent.

Once you've organized your keyword data by themes of search intent, you can sum up the search volume of each theme *and* its subthemes to estimate the number of people searching for those intent topics and prioritize the user tasks you identify accordingly. For example, using pivot tables, we can sum up the themes of pregnancy-related search intent, which makes it possible to see percentage data and helps prioritize user tasks. We list all of the corresponding user tasks for search intent data points alongside any other user tasks identified in other forms of research, too, like user interviews or surveys:

SEARCH INTENT DATA	ALL USER TASKS
Out of seventy-five thousand searches per month:	*Users want to:*
27 percent are looking for waiting-period coverage details	Understand the waiting period
24 percent are looking for health plans that include pregnancy coverage	Find out how my pregnancy medical expenses will be covered by your health plan
17 percent are looking for information on breast pump coverage	Find out if my breast pump is covered under your health plan
10 percent are looking for details on pregnancy coverage while traveling	See what covered birthing facilities look like and the features they offer See if my preferred hospitals and doctors are in your network
8 percent are looking for validation, such as reviews, awards, and ratings	Read reviews and customer ratings
8 percent are looking for cost information	See coverage details Get a quote Sign up for your health plan See if alternative birth centers are covered under your plan Understand the breakdown of average covered costs and how much my part will be

Remember, this isn't an exact science. You'll need to use your best judgment to balance tasks without data, like the ones you have from interviews or surveys, against tasks identified in search intent to best serve your users (and meet your business goals).

Determine your search goals

You'd be surprised how many organizations don't have clear search goals for their site beyond "get more traffic" or "increase conversions." It's even less common to see thoughtfully planned out search goals at the page level. But knowing exactly what to expect from organic search for an individual page, and how it will help achieve business goals, is the only way to avoid chasing vanity metrics.

Although some goals for the health insurance maternity page might be directly tied to search, like "Get organic search visibility for pregnancy health insurance-related terms," others will simply be business goals, like "Help existing plan members learn more about maternity and childbirth coverage and plan options," or "Increase requests for quotes and leads by 15 percent." Use this to discuss how organic search can play a role in helping achieve the page's business goals, and how you will measure its contributions.

Start with the prioritized, measurable business objectives and subobjectives for the page. What does your organization want to achieve with this page? Once known, you can map those objectives back to specific actions or outcomes you can measure in analytics and attribute to organic search. For example, let's look at how business goals for a health insurance website might translate to search goals:

BUSINESS GOALS	SEARCH GOALS
Generate leads from quotes.	Increase the number of quotes generated from organic search traffic.
Connect with people shopping for health insurance for pregnancy.	Rank for "health insurance for pregnancy"-related searches.

BUSINESS GOALS	SEARCH GOALS
Get organic visibility for "health insurance for pregnancy"-related searches.	*This doesn't need any translation, since it's already clearly tied to search.*
Help members understand their pregnancy benefits.	*This doesn't translate well to organic search, since most existing members would visit the site directly to log in to their account or browse the pregnancy page.*
Position ourselves as a leader of pregnancy-friendly health insurance.	Increase organic traffic visits to the blog from the pregnancy page.

Clearly, someone on the team with a little SEO or analytics experience can help with this part. But with a little search knowledge (hey, you're reading this book, right?) and determination, anyone can map business goals to search metrics. We challenge ourselves to list no more than four to six business goals for a single page—more than that, and it becomes hard to effectively work toward any goals.

Inevitably, you might find the business goals you identified and prioritized in the exercise don't directly correlate to user tasks, or, if they do, they might be out of alignment in terms of how you prioritized them. It's not unusual to see business goals for a page that don't map back to any user tasks! Or to see the top priority for users rank at the very bottom of the priorities for the business. That's natural. This exercise is designed to help your group of stakeholders identify misalignments and either realign the business goals to better serve the user's needs or make conscious compromises around them. A *conscious compromise* involves intentionally choosing to prioritize what we want over what users want. (This is clearly not ideal, but at least we can be honest about it and set realistic expectations.) Visualizing these misalignments can be a powerful tool for driving more user-centered design choices.

Choose content elements

Now that you've thought through and prioritized user search goals and tasks, as well as your organization's search goals and general business goals for the page, determine the copy, videos, images, tools, or other elements that will make up the page—and decide what order to present them in.

Have the team list all content they think the page needs to help users accomplish their tasks and your organization achieve its goals, and brainstorm any features or functionality needed to support that content.

Continuing our example of the pregnancy and childbirth page, you might list content elements like this:

- Images of pregnant people, photographs of relevant birthing centers, and pregnancy-related illustrations
- Headline that speaks to "Health Insurance for Pregnancy and Childbirth"
- Brief introductory copy explaining the main benefit of health insurance and outlining what information the user will find on the rest of the page
- Call-to-action banner encouraging readers to get a quote or contact an agent
- Quoting tool or form and submission button
- Content block explaining the waiting-period policy and links to the member login for more in-depth coverage details
- Content block about coverage for breast pumps and lactation consultants with a link for members to log in and explore covered pump options, find covered lactation consultants, or file a claim
- Content block focused on birthing center options, with a mention of both natural childbirth and cesarean birth options
- Graphic illustrating average pregnancy-related medical expenses with health insurance
- Video and text testimonials from members who had their maternity care and childbirth covered by our health plan
- Links to articles on pregnancy and childbirth on the blog

- Links to information on newborn insurance coverage, insurance for pediatric care, and the process of adding a newborn to your health plan

Once you've listed all potential content elements for the page, go back and consider the prioritized business goals and user tasks, and *then* rank the content elements from most to least important. Imagine a user is scrolling through the page on their phone. What's going to show up first? And then next? And then next? All the way down the page.

Whether you're doing this in person with sticky notes, working in a Google doc, or using some kind of online whiteboard collaboration tool, be aware that quite a bit of conversation, even arguing, usually happens during this step. It's common for folks to disagree about which content elements come first, or how best to address the user tasks. It can get rowdy! And that's exactly what you want: people hashing out how they'll address priorities and satisfy search intent now, in the content-planning phase, instead of making expensive page-template changes during development or writing content too close to launch.

What's the best way to do this? Have the team work together to arrange the content elements in a single-column layout (**FIG 4.9**). This forces you and your colleagues to prioritize content, and keeps you focused on content needs rather than on designing elaborate multicolumn layout scenarios, or derailing conversations with visual design decisions.

Consider internal linking structures

Finally, you'll determine the forward paths, the links to where people will go next. These links are essential to the core model's success and should always be considered in the context of the user tasks (and search intent) for the page.

In addition to thinking through general forward paths—like where you want to send the user next, or what documents, downloads, or contact information might be helpful—you'll

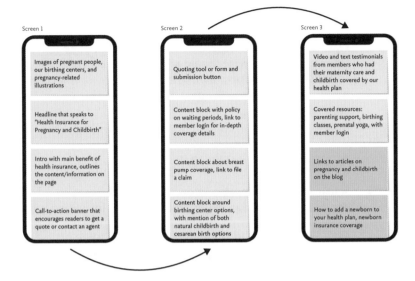

FIG 4.9: Have your team take all brainstormed content types and, in light of prioritized user tasks and business goals, order the content in a single-column layout like this one. We used Miro, an online visual collaboration tool, and had the team order content elements from first to last. The purple stickies at the very end were brainstormed in the next step on internal linking structures.

want to consider how these forward paths impact search visibility. You'll recall from Chapter 3 that forward paths help Google better understand your website overall and the relationships among content components across the site. Forward paths also help Google understand the volume of content and authority you have on a certain subject.

To continue our example, the pregnancy and childbirth page could link to blog posts on pregnancy, articles about childbirth, and coverage details on health insurance for newborns. These forward paths would help search engines better understand the connections between those different types of content and provide users with useful, relevant next steps at multiple phases in their journey.

At the end of this exercise, you should have a clear design artifact that you can use to plan web writing, and that will serve as a foundation for wireframing and template design. Ultimately, this exercise should be equal parts content, design, and SEO—an essential tool for bringing all three together effectively and ensuring search intent will be satisfied before writing even begins.

SCHEMA.ORG MARKUP ELEMENTS

Schema.org markup, also known as *structured data*, is a data vocabulary used by all major search engines for information related to creative work, events, organizations, people, places, and products—as well as different content types such as video, images, or audio. Hundreds of term types let you describe products, publications, local business listings, restaurant menus, and all sorts of industry-specific concepts. While not an official ranking factor for Google, the additional context it provides allows the search engine to show a page in a more relevant context—helping it rank for the right terms (http://bkaprt.com/seo38/04-05).

Beyond communicating data and metadata to Google efficiently, certain types of Schema.org markup can change the appearance of your search results, making content appear on the SERP as starred reviews, product cards, event cards, and more (**FIG 4.10**).

Markup like this helps users better understand what content they can expect from a search result, get answers to their questions more easily, and click through to the most relevant page for their interests (**FIG 4.11**).

Schema.org properties and content elements

You can only include details in your markup that exist as *real details in your web content*. This means Schema.org optimization starts with content planning. You need to account for the right elements in your content and page templates in the design phase, before things go to development. For example, if you

FIG 4.10: SeatGeek uses event markup that helps concerts from our dude, Kurt Vile, listed on its site show up as sublistings under the main page listing on the SERP.

FIG 4.11: This SERP listing shows the product's rating, how many times it has been reviewed, and the price. Schema.org markup makes this possible.

want those sparkly review stars next to your SERP listing, you better have actual third-party reviews on your product page. Beyond having authentic reviews and choosing a reputable third-party review platform, you'll also need to account for how the reviews will be incorporated into the page's design. If you look into the schema types, you'll see the list of elements to mark up has to agree with the list of content you need to include for those page types (**FIG 4.12**).

A word of caution: if you treat this as an afterthought and try to optimize for properties that don't exist in the web content later, your site will get slapped with a penalty from Google (http://bkaprt.com/seo38/04-06).

To get started with Schema.org on your site, research which markup types and properties apply to your content as specifically as possible (http://bkaprt.com/seo38/04-07). Get as granular as you can. Once you determine which Schema.org types apply to your site, explore the content properties for each

Person

A Schema.org Type

Thing > Person

[more...]

A person (alive, dead, undead, or fictional).

Property	Expected Type	Description
Properties from Person		
additionalName	Text	An additional name for a Person, can be used for a middle name.
address	PostalAddress or Text	Physical address of the item.
affiliation	Organization	An organization that this person is affiliated with. For example, a school/university, a club, or a team.
alumniOf	EducationalOrganization or Organization	An organization that the person is an alumni of. Inverse property: alumni
award	Text	An award won by or for this item. Supersedes awards.
birthDate	Date	Date of birth.
birthPlace	Place	The place where the person was born.
brand	Brand or Organization	The brand(s) associated with a product or service, or the brand(s) maintained by an organization or business person.
callSign	Text	A callsign, as used in broadcasting and radio communications to identify people, radio and TV stations, or vehicles.
children	Person	A child of the person.
colleague	Person or URL	A colleague of the person. Supersedes colleagues.
contactPoint	ContactPoint	A contact point for a person or organization. Supersedes contactPoints.

FIG 4.12: These are the Schema.org elements for a person's bio. If you plan to use Schema.org markup for bios on your site, you can use the list of properties in the column on the left as a sort of bio content checklist. Choose applicable elements and include them in your content outline.

FIG 4.13: This is what Schema.org markup for Erika Hall's *Just Enough Research* on the A Book Apart website would look like if implemented.

markup type you're using (**FIG 4.13**). For example, if you wanted to add Schema.org terms to a web page about a book, you would look at the Book type and apply properties like these:

- author, to mark up the author of the book
- numberOfPages, to mark up the number of pages in the book
- datePublished, to mark up the publication date

While you have to plan which Schema.org elements you need to include in your content *now*, in the design phase, Schema.org markup is implemented later on, during the development phase, using JSON-LD in the head of the page. If you're not code-savvy, ask for help from someone in your organization who is. We provide some tips on how to implement this markup during development in Chapter 5.

CONTENT PRODUCTION

Once you've planned content for your page and considered content presentation formats, it's time to tackle the actual writing and on-page optimization. Take heart: having a well-thought-out content plan to address search intent is the hardest part! Now you need to bring that plan to life and make a few search considerations along the way.

As with most aspects of human-centered SEO, there's never really a reason to do something *just* for search engines. SEO is about making things findable for humans, and your web writing and on-page optimizations should reflect this. Here's what to consider when getting your content is ready for prime time.

Incorporate keywords (on-page SEO)

Even though satisfying search intent is the most important thing you can do, you'll still want to set both primary and secondary keyword targets for your page.

Primary keywords are the high-volume, most commonly used search terms that correlate to your high-level themes of search intent. *Secondary keywords* are the high-volume, most commonly used search terms that address all the forms of *subintent* your page addresses. Google's ability to understand synonyms and conceptually related phrases has improved greatly in the past decade, giving us the freedom to use natural language without obsessing over keyword variants (like plurals). This step leverages keyword data to learn more about what language makes the most sense to users and strategically using those terms to optimize on-page elements.

Here are recommendations for incorporating keywords into your content:

- Use primary keywords in the page title, meta description, and main headline (h1 tag) of the page, and in the first few sentences of page copy.
- Use secondary keywords in h2 and h3 tags—for subheadings or section titles that address subintent.
- Be natural. Even when using keywords, write things the way a real human would say them.
- Keyword density doesn't matter, so don't be repetitive if you wouldn't naturally say things more than once.
- Use your search intent research or go back to your keyword research tool to see the most popular ways people describe your products, services, or information, and mirror their language back to them.

Above all, don't focus on using keywords above satisfying the search intent. Your content will need to answer all forms of intent and help users complete their task or solve their problem—regardless of keyword optimization.

Write good meta descriptions and page titles

When you think about the high-priority steps of a user journey, you might think of the homepage or key product pages, the site navigation, or the checkout flow. And you'd be right—these are pivotal moments. But as we've discussed, a good user experience actually starts at the search engine level, where a title and meta description are the only thing between the user and your site.

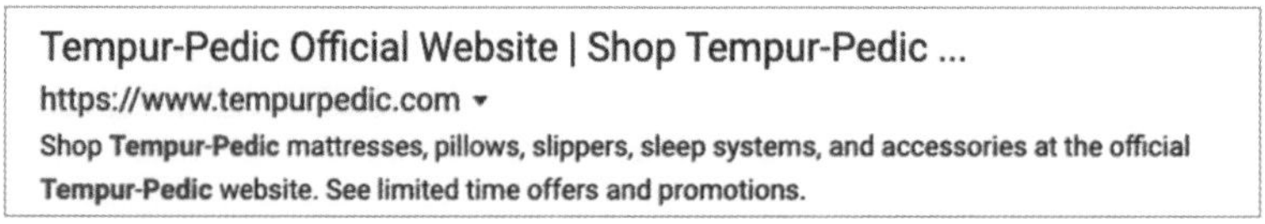

> **Tempur-Pedic Official Website | Shop Tempur-Pedic ...**
> https://www.tempurpedic.com ▾
> Shop **Tempur-Pedic** mattresses, pillows, slippers, sleep systems, and accessories at the official **Tempur-Pedic** website. See limited time offers and promotions.

FIG 4.14: Sure, from this we can tell that Tempur-Pedic sells mattresses and "sleep systems" (whatever that means), but there's nothing to pull us in. Its keyword-crammed description doesn't look like it was written by a real person, and the generic "limited time offers and promotions" is vague.

> **Tuft & Needle: Honest Bed Products that Reinvent Sleep**
> https://www.tuftandneedle.com ▾
> Wake up refreshed after the best night's sleep of your life. Try our online mattresses, sheets, pillows, and frames for 100 nights, with free shipping.

FIG 4.15: This is a helpful, relevant, and specific meta description. Instead of mentioning general promotions, they tell you exactly what to expect: a product trial and free shipping.

For example, take a look at the rather soulless meta description on Tempur-Pedic's homepage (**FIG 4.14**). See how the title is truncated and devoid of personality?

Now, compare that to the meta description from another mattress purveyor, Tuft & Needle (**FIG 4.15**). This time, the headline isn't truncated (it contains just the right amount of text). Furthermore, beyond using the keyword "bed," they add some personality with "honest bed products" and make a bold claim to "reinvent sleep."

The lesson here? To do their job and win the user's click, good titles and meta descriptions must go beyond keywords—they have to be compelling, relevant, on-brand, and helpful. (Keep in mind that click-throughs, over time, can have a positive impact on your ranking overall.) Here are a few guidelines to keep in mind when writing titles and meta descriptions:

- **Stick to the character counts.** Both the title and meta description will be truncated on the SERP if you go over the character-count limits. That's around sixty characters for page titles, and up to 160 characters for meta descriptions.

- **Include keywords.** As discussed in our on-page SEO recommendations, use primary keywords in both the title and meta description whenever possible.
- **Address key search intent.** Make sure your meta description aligns to the key search intent and clearly communicates how your page will help the user achieve their goal.
- **Treat the page title like a headline.** Good headlines don't just describe—they also grab attention, create curiosity, and take a stance. So put on your copywriter hat and craft a page title that stands out.
- **Be specific and honest.** While you want the meta description to be compelling, you don't want to overpromise and under-deliver, or cause confusion by being vague. This can prompt users to hit the back button because they didn't find what they thought they would get based on the description they read. In turn, this could end up hurting your performance metrics over time.
- **Don't overlook brand voice and tone.** Is your brand voice bold, practical, or witty? Does your organization use specific words to describe how your products look, sound, or feel? Meta descriptions, especially those for important, highly visible pages, are places to let that brand voice shine. Be sure to apply any writing guidelines to these.

All right, we're done waxing poetic on titles and meta descriptions. Just remember: meta descriptions and `title` tags for key pages deserve just as much attention as carefully crafted copy on the homepage.

Optimize your images

Images can help convey meaning and, in some cases, satisfy search. A recent study from Jumpshot shows that 20 percent of organic searches consist of Google image searches alone (http://bkaprt.com/seo38/04-08). This shows how important it is to optimize your images for search performance, especially for in-content imagery (as opposed to hero banners or background images). When choosing and preparing images for your site, you should:

- Use semantically relevant file names for the images. For example, if you have an image of an apple tree, the image file name should be something like `apple-tree.jpg`, instead of `img129.jpg`.
- Avoid generic stock images that don't contribute additional meaning to the content. Choose specific images that enhance the text content and can be clearly described to both people and search engines.
- Write descriptive alt text, captions, and copy related to the image, incorporating keywords when appropriate (they should read naturally).
- Look for ways to add value with a helpful chart or diagram when appropriate, since these can help earn visibility in image search results.
- Make sure images are formatted for the web and won't slow down page-load times.

Format for scannability

Nielsen Norman Group (NN/g), which has been running web usability studies for decades, has found that users "scan the pages, trying to pick out a few sentences or even parts of sentences to get the information they want" (http://bkaprt.com/seo38/04-09).

Although we don't think NN/g's assertion that "users do not read on the Web" holds water, we do think it's absolutely true that users scan pages and jump to certain points in the text that align with their interests. Making it easy for people to quickly scan a page and find the information they're looking for is important for search because it means your page has a shot at satisfying their search intent. Otherwise, they're apt to return to Google and search for another page that's easier to read—which ultimately hurts your search rankings.

Here are some of our favorite ways to make content easy to scan:

- Use detailed, descriptive, and accurate headlines to communicate topics immediately.

FIG 4.16: Not only does Healthline make good use of anchor links for a long article page, but it's also clearly on top of researching search intent. These sections are ordered nearly exactly from most to least important search terms.

- If the page is long, use anchor links to give readers an idea of what the page contains and enable them to jump to relevant sections (**FIG 4.16**).
- Highlight critical content in callouts, quotes, or asides.
- Increase the size of heading text appropriately in comparison to the surrounding text. The main `<h1>` heading for the page should be the largest, making the page's main topic obvious to search robots, screen readers, and people.

Showcase expertise

It's ideal for site content to be written by someone with subject-matter expertise, especially when it comes to more nuanced or technical matters. To Google, an author's expertise and verifiable credentials are particularly important for content that impacts people's well-being (http://bkaprt.com/seo38/04-10). Sometimes referred to as Your Money or Your Life (YMYL) content, these topics include news, health, medicine, finance, government, and law, as well as identity issues like ethnicity, religion, disability, gender, and sexual orientation.

Always identify the authors of articles or editorial content on your site. List their credentials, and link to their biographical content, additional publications, connections with other organizations, and social media accounts.

Stay fresh

Fresh, from a search perspective, means content published or updated recently or frequently. Freshness matters to Google—just like it matters to people—when the information is time-sensitive and can impact its relevance, as with news, scientific research, financial advice, and event information. A study published in May 2020 found that "not only do pages where the majority of content changed get crawled more often, but those pages also rank for more keywords" (http://bkaprt. com/seo38/04-11).

This means that part of on-page optimization is keeping content current and updating date-sensitive content as part of your ongoing governance plan. Keep a site inventory spreadsheet containing every URL on your site. Use it to document when pages were last updated (your CMS may allow you to run a report by URLs and their last modified date), make a note of any date- or time-sensitive pages, and plan to update them at regular intervals. This could be quarterly, annually, or even monthly or weekly depending on the context and date relevance of your content.

Adapt voice-and-tone guidelines

Your organization might have guidelines for your brand's voice and tone. Often, these determine the words and phrases your copywriters can use to describe products or services. Such guidelines are excellent for standardizing brand expression, but if they don't take search intent research into account, they can accidentally hinder search and user experience.

For example, our life insurance client ran into trouble aligning their web copy with search intent and user-friendly language because the brand team had developed rules concerning how they would, *and would not*, describe their insurance packages. According to the guidelines, writers were required to use the term *voluntary benefits* rather than *supplementary insurance*, which search intent research showed was used far more by customers and potential customers. The brand guidelines were in direct opposition with how people searched—a real problem for search visibility. A little collaboration between the SEO and brand teams would have resulted in a more effective set of voice-and-tone guidelines that align with the way users actually describe products.

To avoid setting brand guidelines that sound nice but conflict with real user language, use search intent and popular, high-volume keywords as a guide in developing voice and tone. Take it a step further and make sure guidelines go beyond web content, so all marketing copy can reflect consistent, user-friendly terminology, both online and off.

MAKE IT MULTIDISCIPLINARY

By now it is probably obvious that SEO is multifaceted and extends well into information architecture, site navigation, content design, links, images, URLs, and beyond. In the next chapter, we'll talk about some of the more technical aspects of search optimization and discuss how to make sure all the SEO considerations you've put into content and design carry through into how a site is developed.

SEO IN DEVELOPMENT

LET US TELL YOU ABOUT a company that went through a $5 million site redesign but didn't include any SEO considerations. With a hefty investment in user research, they thought they had everything covered. Wow, were they stunned to find out they had lost 40 percent of their traffic and 30 percent of their conversions after the new site launched! Besides not addressing search intent in the new content, they broad-brushed the redirect plan so it overlooked key content, ignored international SEO settings, and locked in the default CMS template settings so the content team couldn't even edit basic search-impacting elements—like `title` tags! It was a real bummer.

With a little knowledge and some technical SEO considerations, that huge drop in performance could have been avoided.

Now, you might be thinking: "Isn't there an SEO plugin for that?" After all, some CMS platforms do have built-in SEO bells and whistles and, sure, there are plugin options for most content management systems that provide some of the SEO scaffolding—saving development time and ensuring precise details are implemented according to search engine standards. But no matter how robust the plugin, it's likely that additional details will need to be considered during development and implementation.

Built-in CMS functionality and plugins are good at providing shortcuts for basic editing needs, like editing titles, URLs, meta descriptions, `noindex` options, and social meta data. They're also great for technical SEO implementation of universal elements, like canonical links, XML sitemaps, and common structured data types. Beyond that, their ability to impact SEO outcomes is limited. Plugins can't guarantee you're using search engine-friendly architecture and semantically meaningful HTML—that's up to you. Identifying the gaps between what you need and what's provided by the platform or plugin is critical, because it allows you to understand what sort of manual implementation efforts will be required during development.

Understanding where technical decisions overlap with SEO performance helps ensure that research and search-friendly design decisions don't get lost in development. You can think of these overlapping areas as *technical SEO*—the practice of improving a site's search visibility through coding and implementation. While you can do a lot to optimize for search in design and content, it needs to live in a sound infrastructure; otherwise, you risk creating an experience that isn't accessible or easily understood by search engines.

TECHNICAL SEO CONSIDERATIONS

Technical SEO isn't just about optimizing your site for crawling and indexing; it's also about how a site is built. It encompasses what can be edited in the CMS, sitemaps, JavaScript indexing, responsive design, and more. Getting technical SEO right is important not only because it helps Google crawl and understand your site more efficiently, but also because the code and technology behind the scenes will ultimately deliver a better, faster, more usable experience for those maintaining and those visiting the website. An improved user experience in the CMS means a less frustrating governance process for content maintainers, leading to better results in the long-term. On the public-facing side, it means people staying on the page longer, interacting further with your site, not clicking the back button, revisiting the site anew, and sharing your content—all boons for SEO.

There's quite a lot to unpack around technical SEO and we don't have the space here to discuss all of its ins and outs—it's a topic deserving of its own book. But we can cover essential requirements that will make sure all of that hard, search-relevant work you did during your research, content, and design phases doesn't get lost in development.

Page titles

A page title is the headline of each search listing that appears as a link in Google search results; it also appears in the browser tab. The text here is contained within the title element in the head of the document. There should only be one instance of a page title per URL. Page titles might seem like an afterthought, but they are highly visible and super important in terms of ranking factor.

Most of the time, CMSs are configured to autogenerate page titles so that titles aren't duplicated or overlooked altogether. This is a good and necessary first step, but since page titles are headlines and their main job is to win the user's click, most of the time they need to be written by a real human.

Although page titles should be editable in the CMS, manually writing page titles for *every single page* on a giant website with hundreds, thousands, or even millions of similar pages can be nearly impossible. To make managing titles for these pages easier, create a pattern for page titles that can be dynamically generated; allow editors to override the automated titles manually if necessary. Some plugins offer this functionality at a base level, but if you're not using plugins, you can implement it on your own.

Whatever route you choose, make sure it results in page titles that are semantically relevant and meaningful to the end user. For example, an effective page title tag might look like this:

```
<title>Shop Jaguar Guitars | Fender</title>
```

An ineffective page `title` tag might look like this:

```
<title>Jaguar</title>
```

Without context, "Jaguar" truly means nothing. It could refer to an animal or a car. That's what you'd get if you simply dropped the page name into `title`.

Meta descriptions

Meta descriptions are the brief (160 characters or fewer) summaries of a page's content that show up in the search engine results underneath the page title. This text is the value of the `content` attribute of the `meta` element with the `name="description"` attribute, in the `head` of the document.

Meta descriptions for each page should be editable in the CMS. It's important not to use overly generalized descriptions as placeholders—when a description is omitted, Google will generate a much more specific and useful one for you, based on the contents of that page. Although this isn't always ideal, it's still better than using duplicate descriptions across multiple pages (**FIG 5.1**).

As with page `title` tags, if you have a high page count for a single type of page, it's possible to create quality autogenerated meta descriptions that emulate well-written sentences. Start with a thoughtful Mad Libs-style template and fill in the blanks with unique data points for that page type. You'll just need to make sure the dynamically inserted data doesn't blow your character count. If you want to build out a really luxe editorial experience and support correct implementation of everything, include some guidance in the CMS on the maximum character count—you could even program functionality that warns users when they go over the character limit. Fancy!

Image optimization

As we discussed in Chapter 4, alt text is a way of describing visual information—our image content. Alt text needs to be easily editable; without it, search engines have trouble under-

www.zillow.com › ... › Tempe › 85282 › Broadmor ▾

325 E Broadway Rd, Tempe, AZ 85282 | MLS #6130484 | Zillow

Zillow has 17 photos of this $425000 3 beds, 2 baths, 1774 Square Feet single family home located at **325 E Broadway Rd, Tempe, AZ 85282** built in 1958.

www.propertyshark.com › ... › Maricopa County ▾

Cheap Homes For Sale in Tempe, AZ - 11 listings

Browse 11 cheap **houses** for sale in **Tempe**, AZ, priced up to $200000. Find cheap **homes** for sale, view cheap condos in **Tempe**, AZ, view real estate listing ...

FIG 5.1: Zillow's page contains organized, contextual, and relevant data points that are pulled together to create a meta description that is helpful, reads naturally, and fits within the character count. PropertyShark's page contains an obvious attempt to keyword-stuff, so its meta description looks robotic and meaningless. Plus, some of the text is truncated because it exceeds the character limit.

standing what images are meant to represent, and that content has no way of showing up in image or video search results. Likewise, images' file names can be interpreted as meaningful content, especially when an `alt` attribute has been omitted. Make sure to implement all images (that aren't purely decorative or only meant as background design) in HTML, and allow editors to manage alt text, captions, and file names in the CMS.

Hyperlinks

Search engines use the language contained in text links to help them understand the purpose of the page referenced by that link. However, while a page's primary content is typically editable by default, microcopy is a frequently overlooked area— smaller content modules, CTA buttons, and other smaller units of content often get designed without the same level of flexibility. Links are often relegated to generic language like "learn more," when a linked headline or a more specific call to action could be much more meaningful to a search engine. Regardless of what you see in mockups and prototypes, give editors the ability to link text anywhere they need to in the content module, not just the button or designated link area. Doing so means you'll need to make sure the link styling doesn't interfere with the module design; you may need to consider a different link style variation. For instance, a headline turning bright blue and underlined on focus could look quite jarring. It might be better to do something subtle, like apply a slight color change on hover instead.

Although they're not in a high-priority location, footer links still have significant influence on how both users and crawlers flow through the site and pass link equity. Editors will need to be able to sculpt this flow on an ongoing basis by having access to edit, add, and remove text links in this area.

Crawling and indexing

Traditionally, technical SEO was all about making sure a site could be crawled (discovered and categorized) and indexed (assessed and then displayed in search results and ranked) by search engines as efficiently as possible. And although that's not the only aspect of technical SEO you need to consider now, it's still really important. As we discussed in Chapter 2, search engines use crawlers to follow links and discover content on your site. Having a solid internal linking structure and avoiding blocking or crawling errors helps Google understand what the most important content is on your site, but there's more to it behind the scenes.

XML sitemaps

An *XML sitemap* is a file created specifically for search engines (as opposed to a dedicated sitemap page intended for users). It lists all of the public-facing URLs on a single domain that should be crawled and indexed for that site, excluding subdomains and any pages like confirmation pages, paywalled or password-protected pages, and landing pages designed specifically for paid-search campaigns. Think of it this way: an XML sitemap is like a map of your website that tells Google where all of the pages are. It helps Google crawl your site more quickly and efficiently.

XML sitemaps should live in the root directory of your site structure (FIG 5.2). Of course, XML sitemaps should be dynamic, automatically updating URLs as they are added to or removed

This XML file does not appear to have any style information associated with it. The document tree is shown below.

```xml
▼<urlset xmlns="http://www.sitemaps.org/schemas/sitemap/0.9">
  ▼<url>
     <loc>http://www.loc.gov/accessibility/</loc>
     <changefreq>weekly</changefreq>
     <priority>0.5</priority>
   </url>
  ▼<url>
     <loc>http://www.loc.gov/accessibility/web-site-accessibility/</loc>
     <changefreq>weekly</changefreq>
     <priority>0.5</priority>
   </url>
  ▼<url>
     <loc>http://www.loc.gov/accessibility/accessibility-for-visitors/</loc>
     <changefreq>weekly</changefreq>
     <priority>0.5</priority>
   </url>
  ▼<url>
     <loc>http://www.loc.gov/accessibility/assistive-technology-for-researchers/</loc>
     <changefreq>weekly</changefreq>
     <priority>0.5</priority>
   </url>
  ▼<url>
     <loc>http://www.loc.gov/accessibility/library-resources/</loc>
     <changefreq>weekly</changefreq>
     <priority>0.5</priority>
   </url>
  ▼<url>
     <loc>http://www.loc.gov/accessibility/library-resources/for-teachers/</loc>
     <changefreq>weekly</changefreq>
     <priority>0.5</priority>
   </url>
```

FIG 5.2: The XML sitemap for the Library of Congress lets search engines know how often they should come back and recrawl. By designating these pages 0.5 on a scale of 0.1 to 1.0 (1.0 being the highest crawl priority), it tells search engines these pages are of medium recrawl priority.

---

from the site. On more sites than you'd like to imagine, you might still find a static sitemap hiding under the hood. These should be set to automatically update, as new pages are added or existing pages are removed. Without setting XML sitemaps to automatically update, they'll quickly fall out of date, often causing more harm or confusion than not having a sitemap at all.

Sitemaps become increasingly important—and impactful— for sprawling sites with higher page counts, since the process of discovering URLs naturally through links becomes increasingly difficult for search engines. Remember, crawlers work by discovering a page and following the links they find *naturally*, like someone browsing the web. On a large site, it could take Google a long time to discover new content crawling naturally like this. An XML sitemap tells Google *exactly* where the new content is so they can index it faster.

```
▼<sitemapindex xmlns="http://www.sitemaps.org/schemas/sitemap/0.9">
  ▼<sitemap>
    <loc>http://www.loc.gov/exhibitions/sitemap.xml</loc>
  </sitemap>
  ▼<sitemap>
    <loc>http://www.loc.gov/librarians/sitemap.xml</loc>
  </sitemap>
  ▼<sitemap>
    <loc>http://www.loc.gov/topics/sitemap.xml</loc>
  </sitemap>
  ▼<sitemap>
    <loc>http://www.loc.gov/accessibility/sitemap.xml</loc>
  </sitemap>
  ▼<sitemap>
    <loc>http://www.loc.gov/subscribe/sitemap.xml</loc>
  </sitemap>
  ▼<sitemap>
    <loc>http://www.loc.gov/books/sitemap.xml</loc>
  </sitemap>
  ▼<sitemap>
    <loc>http://www.loc.gov/connect/sitemap.xml</loc>
  </sitemap>
  ▼<sitemap>
    <loc>http://www.loc.gov/lgbt-pride-month/sitemap.xml</loc>
  </sitemap>
  ▼<sitemap>
    <loc>http://www.loc.gov/education/sitemap.xml</loc>
  </sitemap>
  ▼<sitemap>
    <loc>http://www.loc.gov/help/sitemap.xml</loc>
  </sitemap>
  ▼<sitemap>
    <loc>http://www.loc.gov/classroom-materials/sitemap.xml</loc>
  </sitemap>
  ▼<sitemap>
    <loc>http://www.loc.gov/film-and-videos/sitemap.xml</loc>
  </sitemap>
```

FIG 5.3: The Library of Congress has segmented their sitemaps to correspond to different sections of their site: books, education, LGBT Pride Month, and so on. Segmenting their sitemap like this allows them to get reporting in Google Search Console around those page types, too.

Google limits a single XML sitemap to fifty thousand URLs (and fifty megabytes, uncompressed), so sites with pages over that limit will need to create multiple XML sitemaps linked to from a sitemap index file (FIG 5.3). Some tests show that limiting sitemaps to ten thousand URLs leads to even more thorough levels of indexing (http://bkaprt.com/seo38/05-01).

Once you create your XML sitemap(s), don't forget to submit it (or them) to Google Search Console. Doing so will allow you to keep track of the number of pages Google has indexed from the site, and you can even request a recrawl if you've recently made a lot of updates. To make it easy to manage sitemaps and measure crawling/indexing progress, it's a good idea to segment

URLs into multiple sitemaps by the type of URL, content, or section (or whatever kind of segmentation is important within the context of your site). For example, you might have one XML sitemap with articles, another with product pages, and so on. With only one file, you can't see which pages are and aren't indexed.

Robots.txt

If the main purpose of an XML sitemap is to tell engines where you do want them to crawl, the primary purpose of a robots. txt file is to suggest where you *don't* want them to crawl. We say "suggest" quite literally here, because sometimes Google blows through these stop signs.

Robots.txt is the plain text file part of the *robots exclusion protocol*, a standard used by websites to communicate with web crawlers and other web robots. It operates on basic "disallow" and "allow" commands, giving you the ability to clearly communicate which pages or directories you'd like crawlers not to follow so those pages won't likely get indexed if you don't want them to (**FIG 5.4**).

Robots.txt files are best for:

- Keeping non-public-facing content private. This is essentially a backup plan; it doesn't replace site security if you allow people to access these files without security in front of them, like in an admin or staging area.
- Preventing new content (like a page behind a paywall) from being discovered and indexed.
- Stopping internal search results pages from showing in SERPs.
- Setting crawl delays for specific bots that are overloading the server (though we don't suggest limiting crawling for Google or Bing, since that could adversely impact indexing).
- Specifying the location of your XML sitemap(s). The file is located in the root directory of a site. So, for site www. example.com, you would find the file at www.example.com/ robots.txt.

```
←  →  C    🌐 https://www.example.com/robots.txt

User-agent: *
Disallow:

Sitemap: https://www.example.com/sitemap.xml
```

```
←  →  C    🌐 https://www.example.com/robots.txt

User-agent: *
Disallow: /

Sitemap: https://www.example.com/sitemap.xml
```

FIG 5.4: On the left is an example of a robots.txt file that allows all bots (*) to crawl all locations of the site and specifies the location of the XML sitemap. On the right, the addition of the "/" after the "Disallow:" command blocks crawling of every page on the site. Proceed with caution—the most detrimental mistake you can make in SEO is accidentally blocking your entire site from crawls.

It's important to note that a robots.txt file influences crawling, not indexing. Restricting access in the robots.txt file prevents crawlers from discovering the content in the first place. However, if the content has *already* been discovered by a crawler before you had the robots.txt file in place, restricting access in the file won't remove it from the index. If you want to block engines from *indexing* content, the better choice is to implement a noindex tag directly on those pages. That way, they won't show up in search results at all.

noindex tags

Although you most likely want nearly all of the pages on your site indexed by engines, there may be a few you don't (like a special offer for existing customers or PDF content you don't

	Duplicate Page Examples	Preferred, Canonical URL
Adding "www."	https://www.example.com/page	
http not https	http://example.com/page	
Use of an alternate version	https://example.com/page/overview	https://example.com/page
Capital letter	https://example.com/Page/	
Adding a trailing slash	https://example.com/page/	
Analytics tracking parameters	https://example.com/page?utm=top-nav	

FIG 5.5: Here's an example of how even slight variations to a single URL can end up creating multiple pages in Google's eyes. In cases like this, select one version of each URL, implement canonical tags linking only to that preferred version, and then consistently link to the same version in navigation, footer, content, and XML sitemap(s).

want to show up in search). Adding a `noindex meta` tag in the `head` of that page will get the job done.

We recommend not making this editable in the CMS to protect your site from folks accidentally applying `noindex` to meaningful pages.

URL styling

Even slight inconsistencies in URLs—such as trailing slashes, *http* rather than *https*, a capital letter instead of a lowercase, or the addition of tracking parameters—will be parsed as a unique URL or page by a search engine, even if they are the same pages with the same content (**FIG 5.5**). Referencing multiple URL versions of the same page leads to duplicate content issues in a search engine's index and dilutes the link authority of each page. Linking to multiple variations of the same page divides PageRank into smaller increments across several URLs, rather than consolidating that power under one more authoritative URL. Duplicate pages can also wreak havoc in analytics reporting, making it difficult to view the total performance of a page in one line or row of data.

Piggybacking off the work we did in Chapter 4, to design URLs that communicate site structure and subject matter relevance, there are additional technical details you will need to consider to avoid duplicate content and to consolidate authority (and performance) under one URL.

Identify and document the URL format your organization prefers. Our recommendations:

- Stick with all lowercase letters.
- Use hyphens ("-") as word separators because they are great for user and search engine readability.
- There are no SEO advantages or downsides to starting your URLs with *www*, or ending them with a trailing slash. The important part is that you stick with one and use it consistently.
- Choose the secure *https* option. Most browsers now show warnings for non-secure content, and secure URLs give you a slight ranking boost.

Once you've implemented your URL system, link only to preferred URLs for each page from all site locations: navigation, footer, in-content links, calls to action, and your XML sitemap(s).

To properly cement your preferred URL decisions in stone, implement canonical tags. A canonical tag (`<link rel="canonical" href="https://example.com/page"/>`) is an HTML element added to the `head` of the page that allows you to communicate the exact version of the URL you'd like the search engine to index. If a search engine were to happen upon a duplicate version of that page, the canonical sends a strong suggestion to the engine to index only the preferred, canonical version. Reference "Canonical Tags: A Simple Guide for Beginners" from Ahrefs for more details (http://bkaprt.com/seo38/05-02).

Canonical tags are a suggestion, but not a directive, to search engines. For a bulletproof backup plan, implement a 301 redirect for non-preferred versions to go to the preferred ones. For example, let's say you decide all URLs will not end in a trailing slash ("/"). Redirect anybody trying to access a version with the trailing slash to the preferred version, the one without the slash.

For sites that have already adequately set their canonicals and currently drive significant levels of organic search traffic, be careful about making any changes to the URLs. One small update can change all URLs for the entire site, creating the need for a search engine to reindex all pages, which will cause a disruption in search visibility. It may be worth timing any URL changes with other major changes—like a site redesign or a migration—to minimize the number of times your URLs will change.

Pagination

Site pagination lists and links the pages within a given site section, such as onsite search results, category pages, or forum threads. Pagination is a clever sleight of hand that ensures there are crawlable links to deeper content on the site, so that users and search engines alike can discover all of the content in every section.

Before jumping headfirst into pagination, determine if you need it at all. If there are only a few items in a category, it is often faster and more straightforward to present all of the items on one page, rather than splitting them into paginated results. But if presenting all items at once would overwhelm users or slow load times down, pagination is a good option.

Here are the two best search-friendly ways to paginate:

- **Multipage links.** This is the most common style of pagination, where each page in the series is linked from a numbered list (**FIG 5.6**). This is a solid (if no-frills) approach that makes it easy for search engines to understand, and easy for users to browse and return to the listings. This method uses *self-referencing canonicals,* where the canonical link for each page links to itself.
- **View more.** This method allows users to load the next set of results within the original item listing (**FIG 5.7**). This is a good option when you want to encourage users to continue browsing all results (as with a retail store shopping experience) but still want to make it easy for them to stay oriented within a specific set of items. This method also uses self-referencing canonicals.
- **Infinite scroll.** This method loads additional content as the user scrolls down the page, essentially eliminating pagination. Although infinite scroll has enjoyed some popularity, it has many hidden downsides for both search engines and

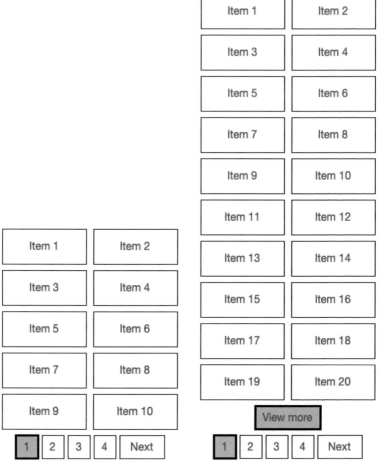

FIG 5.6: With multipage linking, the item series displays self-referencing canonical links to provide access to subsequent pages in the series.

FIG 5.7: In this wireframe example, a user has clicked the "View more" button to display a second set of ten items beneath the first set.

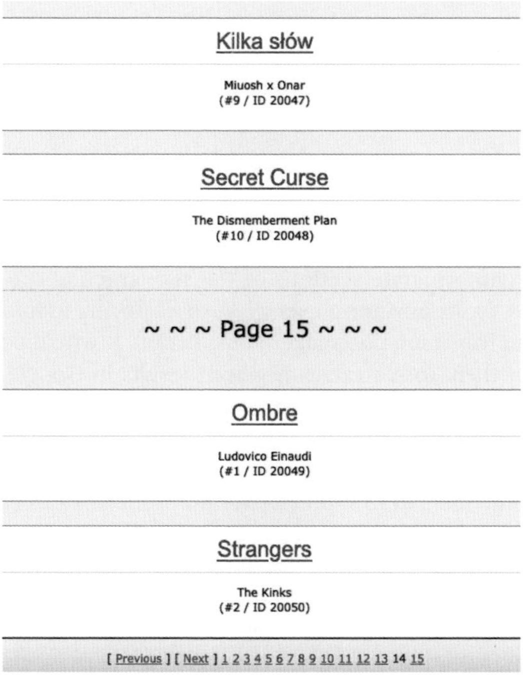

Kilka słów

Miuosh x Onar
(#9 / ID 20047)

Secret Curse

The Dismemberment Plan
(#10 / ID 20048)

~ ~ ~ Page 15 ~ ~ ~

Ombre

Ludovico Einaudi
(#1 / ID 20049)

Strangers

The Kinks
(#2 / ID 20050)

[Previous] [Next] 1 2 3 4 5 6 7 8 9 10 11 12 13 14 15

FIG 5.8: John Muller built this example site to show how multipage linking can be incorporated into infinite scrolling (http://bkaprt.com/seo38/05-05). Here, the multipage links indicate placement on page 14, which will change as page 15 scrolls to the top of the screen.

users. Currently, search engines can't crawl content that isn't present on page load, so everything that loads with the scroll is essentially invisible. Infinite scroll can also make users feel like they're not in control of the experience, and can make it maddeningly difficult to find particular content (like the footer) (http://bkaprt.com/seo38/05-03). If you must implement endless scrolling, tread very carefully. John Muller, a senior webmaster trends analyst at Google, recommends including multipage links with infinite scroll (**FIG 5.8**), and automatically updating the URL to the next page in the series as users scroll down (http://bkaprt.com/seo38/05-04).

When you talk about pagination, inevitably someone will bring up pagination markup. Although Google no longer uses this markup (rel="next" and rel="prev"), it *can* provide way-finding hints to users browsing via assistive technologies—

especially with a markup pattern that is difficult to parse but essential for navigating a site. This markup is also relevant to frontend performance, potentially allowing modern browsers to preemptively queue up requests for related assets.

International SEO

Imagine a website for a global organization that distributes pacemakers, with separate sections of the site targeting specific countries. Now, imagine a user in Australia trying to find a doctor for an in-person pacemaker consultation. It would be frustrating for them to see relevant search results in Google, only to click through to information on how to book a consultation in the United States. And if there's no visual cue to indicate what region the user is currently viewing? No helpful message to guide them to the appropriate site section? Painful.

This is exactly the kind of thing that happens to users when hreflang is ignored or set up improperly. If you work with multilingual sites or sites targeted to multiple countries, you'll want to use hreflang—an HTML attribute that specifies the language and geographical targeting of a web page—to help Google understand your intended audience location and language. If you have multiple versions of a page for different languages or regions, hreflang annotations tell search engines about the relationship among those alternate versions to make sure the right version of the page—in the right language, targeted to people in the right geographic area—shows up in search results.

These attributes can be implemented through code placed either directly in the head of each regional page, in your XML sitemap(s), or in HTTP headers. You'll want the markup to list all URLs that are alternates or regional equivalents to one another, the language referenced on the page, and the country target for each URL, including the URL for the page you're adding markup to. Keep in mind that it's fine to specify a language by itself, but never a region by itself.

As an example, in this markup we're setting the United States version of the homepage as the global default, meaning it's the page you'd want users from all other countries to find:

```
<head>
  <title>Your Organization, Inc.</title>
  <link rel="alternate" hreflang="en-US"
        href="https://www.yourorganization.com" />
  <link rel="alternate" hreflang="es-US"
        href="https://www.yourorganization.com/es"
  />
<link rel="alternate" hreflang="en-GB"
        href="https://www.yourorganization.com/uk"
  />
<link rel="alternate" hreflang="zh-hans-HK"
        href="https://www.yourorganization.com/hk/
  zh" />
<link rel="alternate" hreflang="en-HK"
        href="https://www.yourorganization.com/hk/
  en" />
  <link rel="alternate" hreflang="de-DE"
        href="https://www.yourorganization.com/de"
  />
  <link rel="alternate" hreflang="x-default"
        href="https://www.yourorganization.com" />
</head>
```

You might have noticed the regions here are capitalized—these are *technically* case-insensitive, but uppercasing the region is a common practice.

Implementation of hreflang is complex, difficult to perfect (especially when you have a large enterprise site with millions of pages), and hinges on having a consistent site structure and aligned implementation governance between each regional or language section. In other words, hreflang is complicated because it requires multiple people managing different sites to follow the same steps in a coordinated fashion, as well as someone to monitor the implementation on an ongoing basis to ensure the protocols are being followed. If you're in a position to champion this cause, or know someone in your organization who is, remember it's a worthwhile endeavor and an important part of international SEO. See the Resources section for more information on hreflang implementation.

JavaScript SEO

Avoid JavaScript rendering for core content or key areas of a site. If you must use it, be sure to provide backup dynamic rendering (prerendering) for search engines with a static HTML version of the page, and make sure your site's `robots.txt` file doesn't disallow crawling of your JavaScript files.

Testing has shown that content in JavaScript can take days or weeks to be crawled and indexed, resulting in lower search visibility; static HTML rendering is always the faster route (http://bkaprt.com/seo38/05-06). Currently, Google and Bing can index JavaScript-rendered content (although we're not sure to what degree Bing can). Yandex and Baidu have limited support, and other engines have little to no support for JavaScript.

In his article "The Ultimate Guide to JavaScript SEO," Tomek Rudzki notes that despite JavaScript's popularity, many JavaScript websites "underperform in Google because they don't do JavaScript SEO properly." Bottom line: even the "best" JavaScript rendering frameworks can deprioritize semantic markup and frontend performance in ways that impact SEO (http://bkaprt.com/seo38/05-07). This is about as technical as SEO gets—we highly recommend you check out Rudzki's guide to avoid any potential issues early on.

Develop a device-agnostic website

Historically, Google's index relied on how your site performed when rendered on desktop devices, and the content displayed there, when evaluating the relevance of a page to a user's query. Now, since the majority of users access Google with a mobile device, Googlebot primarily crawls and indexes a website using the mobile-rendered version of the site's content. So if users can't access the same content on small screens that they can on desktop devices, via a fast-loading, user-friendly experience, you're in trouble.

A thoughtful approach to responsive design is your best bet here. You need to offer the same content (including text, images, videos, links, and structured data and metadata) regardless of the device being used to access the site or the screen size it's

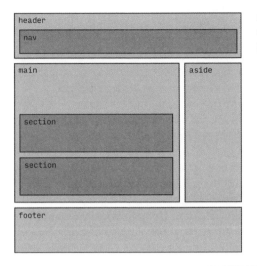

FIG 5.9: This wireframe shows what HTML5 sectioning on a page can look like.

being rendered on. Treating the mobile view of your website as an afterthought, or creating a secondary mobile site with pared-down content or a separate "streamlined" mobile experience, poses a risk to your rankings because Google indexes the web on a mobile-first basis, regardless of whether or not you have a mobile-friendly experience.

Use tags to structure pages

Markup plays a significant role in how your site is understood by any technology tasked with parsing a page for meaning, from search engines to assistive technologies like screen readers. HTML's sectioning elements (header, nav, main, section, aside, and footer, to name a few) allow you to utilize specifically named containers to add essential context to the sections of a page that can't be conveyed by the content alone, and clearly signal where one part of the page ends and another begins (**FIG 5.9**).

Well-formed markup communicates not only the role of each section of a page, but also its relative importance and how it relates to other sections. For example, drawing a clear boundary around the core content of a page allows crawlers to better understand its primary focus. A properly coded page will make it clear that an individual blog post's most important content is the post itself, inside a `main` element, not the supplemental content—advertisements, author contact information, and so on—wrapped in an `aside` element that has been styled as the post's sidebar.

Heading elements

Heading elements play a key role in communicating the structure of a page and defining the relationship between the pieces of content above and below the headings. They provide a way to outline the contents of the page with a clear hierarchy ranging from `h1` through `h6`.

For on-page SEO, the advice has traditionally been to use headings hierarchically throughout a page's content, where `h1` represents the top headline on the page used to describe the main topic, and subsections organized from `h2` through `h6` represent the subtopics. This came about because headings communicate the meaning and context of a page, which is of great interest to search engines. While that still holds true, search engines have evolved and gotten much better at parsing meaning in more advanced ways. This is important because headings are about more than content—ultimately, they're about usability. In order to make sure your pages are accessible to *everyone*—especially folks using screen readers and other accessibility devices—you can't just apply header tags to the content. You have to use them to give context to the whole page and all of its elements, from navigational elements to the logo.

The HTML specification also allows each sectioning element to have its own heading outline (`h1` through `h6` inside of each `article`, for example)—no more or less correct on paper than a page-level outline. In theory, this pattern might someday allow for individual sections of a page to be syndicated to external sources while retaining a sensible internal heading structure. In practice, however, this is where things can break down for users navigating with assistive technology. It can be especially problematic for people using built-in keyboard shortcuts to quickly navigate via headings—not just within a page's content, but the page itself. Make sure you use heading elements to communicate the structure of the entire page, beyond just the content elements, to make it clear to both users and search engines what your page and its content are about. And it goes without saying that we should use heading elements only to communicate meaning, not for styling or any other purpose.

Site speed, responsiveness, and visual stability

Site performance is one of the few subjects where Google is forthcoming about impact on search results: fast, well-built sites rank better, full stop. Performance matters to Google because it matters to users—so much so that the company created metrics around site speed, responsiveness, and visual stability known as Core Web Vitals (http://bkaprt.com/seo38/05-08).

Core Web Vitals aim to measure overall site performance, and are made up of three specific measurements:

1. *Largest Contentful Paint* (LCP) looks at how quickly a page renders its largest image or text in the initial viewport. You should aim for this initial content to load in under 2.5 seconds (http://bkaprt.com/seo38/05-09).
2. *First Input Delay* (FID) measures load responsiveness, or the time it takes the browser to respond to user interaction with the page. Here, you'll want to be under a hundred milliseconds (http://bkaprt.com/seo38/05-10).
3. *Cumulative Layout Shift* (CLS) measures the visual stability of the page by summing up each and every unexpected layout shift that wasn't caused by user interaction. With this one, your target score is 0.1 or less (http://bkaprt.com/seo38/05-11).

Ensuring that your site is doing everything it can to deliver a fast, responsive, visually stable experience can make all the difference. Here are a few tools that can help you optimize for Core Web Vitals and site performance in general:

- **Google Search Console** can give you a bird's eye view of how your pages are performing according to its Core Web Vitals. It categorizes each URL as *poor, needs improvement,* or *good* (**FIG 5.10**).

FIG 5.10: A Core Web Vitals report in Google Search Console. This site is in bad shape: the majority of its URLs fall into Google's "poor" category. Ideally, as you implement improvements to your site, you should see this report improve.

- **Google Analytics Site Speed** reports allow you to pinpoint pages that load slowly. It will show your site's average load speed across different dimensions to see how quickly your pages loaded over a set period of time, in different browsers, or in specific countries. And Page Timing reports will let you know which pages are slowing you down most often, too (**FIG 5.11**).
- Google's **PageSpeed Insights** tool (http://bkaprt.com/seo38/05-12) gives you page-by-page performance scores from Google (**FIG 5.12**) and recommendations on how to improve those scores (**FIG 5.13**). It measures loading, interactivity, and visual stability metrics (part of Google's Core Web Vitals) for your site.

FIG 5.11: The Google Analytics Page Timings report shows you URLs with loading-speed issues so you can pinpoint where to make improvements.

FIG 5.12: Google PageSpeed Insights provides an overview of how a page is performing with a handful of Core Web Vitals metrics.

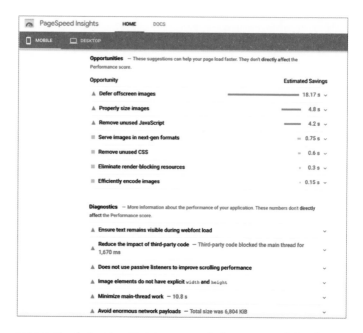

FIG 5.13: Google PageSpeed Insights suggests further recommendations for improving your page performance.

STRUCTURED DATA IMPLEMENTATION

As discussed in Chapter 4, Schema.org is a structured-data markup schema used by all major search engines for information pertaining to creative work, events, organizations, people, places, and products. Using this on-page markup (implemented in JSON-LD) helps search engines better understand the information on a page. Correct implementation from a technical perspective is imperative. Not implementing structured markup according to guidelines will either trigger errors in your code, causing a search engine to ignore your markup altogether, or, worse, will cause your site to be penalized. Here are a few tips:

- Stay away from marking up information in your structured data that doesn't correspond to content literally represented on that page.
- Future-proof your implementation by using Google's preferred method, JSON-LD. While JSON-LD can be implemented anywhere in the page, studies have shown that incorporating the code in the head is most commonly validated by Google (http://bkaprt.com/seo38/05-13).
- Visit Google's official list of structured data it supports for use in rich snippets to understand how the markup could impact the visual display of your SERP listing (http://bkaprt.com/seo38/05-14).

For more details on creating error-free Schema.org code, check out the Schema.org website and Google's "General Structured Data Guidelines" (http://bkaprt.com/seo38/05-15).

How to treat Schema.org markup in the CMS is complex. The world is still really figuring out the best way to enable editors to manage this without dev resources, and there isn't yet a perfect solution. Most solutions we see require technical implementation or use of a plugin. Editors might not need to change this markup often, but someone dedicated to SEO in your organization likely will. While it takes dev resources to set up Schema.org in the background, building the capability to edit certain markup fields in the CMS so SEO specialists and adventurous content editors can update it themselves—instead of relying on dev resources to make one-off changes—could be a huge time-saver.

As we outlined in Chapter 4, someone working with content will need to determine which Schema.org markup is appropriate, and which pages it will apply to, before developers can implement it and create an editing interface in the CMS to support this markup.

REDIRECT IMPLEMENTATION

If you lose a ton of traffic after a redesign that involved changes to URLs, taxonomy, navigation, or any of the like, your first step should always be to review the redirect implementation. Chances are a lot of URLs have changed and now you've got a bunch of broken links—where links in search results and from other sites linking to you result in a 404 error for the user. This is no trifle. As Tim Berners-Lee said in his brilliant piece from 1998, "Cool URIs Don't Change":

> When you change a [URL] on your server, you can never completely tell who will have links to the old [URL]. They might have made links from regular web pages. They might have bookmarked your page. They might have scrawled the [URL] in the margin of a letter to a friend. (http://bkaprt.com/seo38/05-16)

When links break, frustration abounds; usability is impeded. Furthermore, in our experience, sites that don't take seamless redirects seriously during a site transition will lose anywhere from 40 to 85 percent of their organic traffic. Search engines simply aren't set up to make the connection between your older previously ranked pages and the new content you're launching. All the search value from those old pages, in terms of the content and the link authority they had, gets lost instead of being transferred to the new related pages, and old URLs could still show up in SERPs.

The first takeaway here is that you shouldn't change URLs if you don't need to—although sometimes they *must* be changed, because they weren't created with semantic relevance in mind. The second takeaway is that anytime significant changes are made to a site's domain location, content, information architecture, navigation, design, or functionality, there's a risk of losing the organic visibility the site has already earned.

It's during this transition from old pages to new pages, or the old site experience to the new one (also known as site migration), that a plan on how to handle redirects becomes really important. We call this a *redirect guide*.

During site migration, it's important to establish a redirect strategy that gives users and search engine bots alike a seamless experience when attempting to access URLs from the previous site. Think of a redirect guide as a tool to send users and search engine crawlers to a new URL where the content satisfies the same intent as closely as possible.

The complexity of your redirect plan will depend largely on the complexity of the project. If you're doing a complete site redesign—one where most URLs will change, pages will be eliminated and added, multiple properties will merge into one domain, or the domain name itself will change—your plan will be fairly involved. But even a single change in a single URL can still benefit from a (simpler) redirect plan.

Whatever your situation may be, creating a redirect plan will help minimize (or eliminate) poor post-migration search performance and ensure as smooth of a transition as possible for users and search engines.

Types of redirects

The most common types of redirects are 301 (a permanent redirect), 302 (a temporary redirect where the HTTP method can change), and 307 (a temporary redirect where the HTTP method must remain the same). A 301 redirect is considered the most SEO-friendly redirect; it communicates to a search engine that this URL has *permanently* moved to a new location. Because the decision is permanent, search engines understand you won't be changing this again anytime soon, so they remove the old URL from their index and add the new one.

A 302 or 307 redirect communicates to search engines that the move is *temporary*. Therefore, they do not remove the old URL from their index or transfer link equity from the old page to the new.

Some Google employees have stated that Google now passes the same levels of link equity (or PageRank, Google's patented term) between 301s, 302s, and 307s (http://bkaprt.com/seo38/05-17). But industry tests show otherwise. In a 2016 Moz article, Mike King explained:

[A client] had millions of links both internally and externally pointing to URLs that returned 302 response codes. After many meetings, and a more compelling business case, the one substantial thing that we were able to convince them to do was switch those 302s into 301s. Nearly overnight there was an increase in rankings. (http://bkaprt.com/seo38/05-18)

The lesson here? The only time you should use a 302 or 307 redirect is when a URL moves locations for a brief time, as when A/B testing or when adding a temporary alternate version of a page without impacting the rankings of the original page. Otherwise, stick to 301 redirects.

Avoid redirect chains

A *redirect chain* happens when there is more than one redirect between the original URL and the final destination. Redirect chains can lead to slower load times, especially in mobile browsing contexts, and slow load times can block search engines from acknowledging the redirect altogether. If a search engine is unable to take note of the redirect, it won't pass link authority to the new URL, nor will it switch the old URL out for the new one in search results.

Redirect chains are also more difficult to maintain from a content management perspective. All it takes is for someone to forget or mistype one URL in a chain, and *whammo*—you've got yourself a dead link.

Google stated in 2014 that it can follow a maximum of five redirect links in a chain (http://bkaprt.com/seo38/05-19). They recommend linking directly to the final destination or, if that's not possible, minimizing the steps in the chain to three or fewer. Ultimately, redirect chains are usually the result of a lack of governance around redirects and legacy sites. It's best to clean them up and try to eliminate chains entirely.

Manual versus automated redirects

The best way to handle redirects is at the page level: assigning each outdated URL a new URL that satisfies the *same search*

From	To
phoenixzoo.org/africa-trail.asp	phoenixzoo.org/explore/trails/africa-trails
phoenixzoo.org/monkeys.asp	phoenixzoo.org/explore/animals/monkeys
phoenixzoo.org/mandrill.asp	phoenixzoo.org/explore/animals/monkeys/mandrill
phoenixzoo.org/giraffe.asp	phoenixzoo.org/explore/animals/giraffe
phoenixzoo.org/contact.asp	phoenixzoo.org/contact-us
phoenixzoo.org/accessibility.asp	phoenixzoo.org/visit/accessibility
phoenixzoo.org/store/shirt?id=3472	phoenixzoo.org/gift-shop/adult-otter-nonsense-tee
phoenixzoo.org/store/shirt?id=3473	*Product no longer available, let die in 404*
blog.phoenixzoo.org/zoo-news/deer-diary/	phoenixzoo.org/blog/deer-diary
blog.phoenixzoo.org/safari-zoo-animal-stories/	*Article not migrated, let die in 404*

FIG 5.14: Redirecting at the page level ensures you're meeting user expectations, aligning new pages with the original search intent, and transferring SEO value to the new URL.

intent as the original page (**FIG 5.14**). Mapping your redirect decisions on a page-by-page basis can be tedious and time-consuming work, especially when there are hundreds or thousands of URLs at stake—but it is seriously worth every minute of your time. Ignoring page-level redirects or taking shortcuts is a good way to damage search rankings post-migration.

A common shortcut we see clients try to take is applying the same redirect to many pages at once, such as redirecting all old URLs to the new homepage. That might save time up front, but it'll cost you—in both search rankings and user experience—in the long run. Blanket redirects force users to start their search process from scratch or navigate through an unfamiliar site structure in search of specific content. Search engines treat blanket redirects as soft 404s—you likely know 404s as error pages, but they can also serve to direct users to pages that aren't comparable to the old content. Google won't transfer link equity from the old to the new location, and your site will lose what equity it had built.

We once worked on a migration strategy during a site redesign for a large ecommerce website. All URLs were changing in the process, meaning there would be over four million different URLs in the redirect plan!

Obviously, making redirect decisions for four million URLs one at a time would be unthinkable—so we sought out ways to automate decisions as often as possible. One page type on the site accounted for 99 percent of the URL count and 75 percent of the site's organic search traffic: the product pages. Getting redirects right for these pages was essential to a successful migration. The development team was able to implement a dynamic solution that implemented automatic 301 redirects for each of the old product URLs to the new equivalent product URL—and without any redirect chains, to boot!

While we had a workable solution for product pages, there were still other page types we needed to account for—product category pages, manufacturer pages, articles, and more. We determined there was no way to automate redirects for these URLs, so we handled the remaining several hundred redirects by documenting our redirect decisions one at a time in a spreadsheet. The development team then used the spreadsheet to update the site's `.htaccess` file (where redirect lists are officially entered).

The combination of dynamic and manual redirect solutions ensured we accounted for all URL changes in the site redesign. At launch, there was no short-term loss in organic traffic or conversions while Google crawled, indexed, and processed the new changes. By incorporating SEO strategy into the design, development, and site migration process, the site experienced a 50 percent increase in traffic and a 74 percent increase in revenue from organic search in the first year, post-launch. Success!

Perhaps yours isn't a complex ecommerce site, or a property with such a high page count. For most projects, creating a spreadsheet to document all of your redirect decisions will be fairly straightforward, and can be repurposed by your development team during the implementation process.

Don't be afraid of 404s

Some people get nervous at the thought of letting their outdated content lead to a 404 (page not found) response. In an effort to keep users on the site and not lose their business, these nervous folks push to have outdated URLs redirect to the home page. But there's nothing wrong with a page-not-found error as long as it's the result of a purposeful decision, not an accident or oversight. On the contrary, letting a page die in a 404 response is incredibly useful to users and search engines, clearly communicating that the content is no longer available.

If you go this route, make sure the server is configured to return a 404 status code for these pages—that way, you send a clear signal to engines that this URL is longer available and that they should remove it from their index.

Okay, that's it. Bet you never imagined going so deep into redirects, right?

CHECK YOURSELF

It's always helpful for the whole team to talk things through in person before development starts. Try a working session with representation from design, development, and content to walk through the requirements together. Discuss the expected functionality of wireframes or design comps from an editorial standpoint. Think through which elements of each content module will need to be editable, and whether those changes will occur at the site or page level. This decreases the likelihood of unforeseen misunderstandings in implementation and gets everyone on the same page.

Up to this point, we've focused on making search-friendly design decisions and bringing them to life with the right technical considerations in development and editorial tools in the CMS. We've discussed *what* needs to happen for human-centered SEO; in the next chapter, we'll explore *how* we'll get the buy-in and implement the workflow it takes to get it done. There's so much opportunity for more efficient coordination between SEO, UX, and content—the key is making sure we create room in our process for it to happen.

6 SEO IN YOUR ORGANIZATION

AS SENIOR VICE PRESIDENT of marketing and product at Healthline Media, Tracy Rosecrans led a redesign that turned them into the fastest-growing health information site in the United States—more than doubling their search traffic in the span of a year (**FIG 6.1**).

How'd they do it? Rosecrans explained:

> *Our overarching philosophy...that has guided our success has been [to] provide the best content...and the best user experience for every [search] query. We take user experience very seriously, to the point where we have a cross-functional team from product, editorial, marketing, and engineering that meets on a weekly basis...[We ask ourselves,] "What can we test to improve overall user engagement?" (http://bkaprt.com/seo38/06-01)*

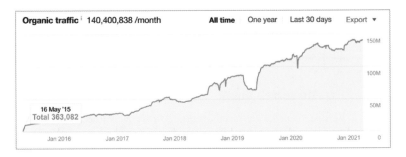

FIG 6.1: Following a redesign that emphasized the user experience and relied on search data to inform the site's content strategy, Healthline has seen continued growth of organic search traffic. (Traffic estimate generated using Ahrefs.)

Ultimately, for Healthline, it all came down to using data, UX, and SEO to inform the site's content strategy. By improving the entire site experience, they boosted their search rankings and earned all of that traffic.

What Rosecrans and the team at Healthline understood was that you can't really "do" SEO in isolation from the rest of the web design process. Trying to optimize for search after the design is done creates a lot of unnecessary redoubling of work. Creating space for SEO earlier, and getting the resources and time it takes to do it right, will save you time and heartache down the line. Just be aware that it takes a lot of effort and preparation up front.

In this chapter, we'll explore ways to earn support for organic search projects, communicate the value of SEO, make space for human-centered SEO in your organization, and measure search performance to sustain the support you need for the long haul.

GETTING BUY-IN

Buy-in: the magical ingredient that makes everything work. At its core, buy-in is *belief*. When people are bought-in, they have confidence in the value of the time and effort invested in the endeavor. They clear roadblocks, find budget, and make space. If you want to get anywhere with human-centered search in your organization, you're going to need that kind of buy-in from executives, stakeholders, and team members—and you're going to have to *earn* it.

Explain search intent

Before you can get folks on board with the value of SEO, they have to understand what it is and how it works in the first place. It's likely that people within your organization will have a slightly different understanding of what modern SEO entails. Satisfying search intent over more classic forms of SEO, like keyword targeting, may feel unfamiliar to some. You will need to make sure the group has a baseline understanding of how modern search works with the overall user experience in order for them to seriously consider setting aside resources and budget for SEO.

Gather a few talking points, perhaps in a deck, that illustrate what modern search is all about. Whatever you do, be sure to emphasize how satisfying search intent plays a critical role in visibility as well as user experience. If stakeholders don't understand what search intent is or why it's important, they won't be able to prioritize it, and all of your hard-earned insights will go unused.

Do a demo

Doing a "search demo" can also be an efficient, powerful way to engage stakeholders with SEO. Demonstrating how search works, in real time and on your real site, can reveal challenges with the current search experience and highlight the importance of satisfying search intent.

Think about some of the most critical search queries, the ones your organization expects to rank for, and questions your users might have—especially questions tied to the products, services, or information that your organization isn't currently getting visibility for. It's helpful to tie the search queries both to business goals and to real user needs that show emotion, like urgency or frustration. Authentic, relatable scenarios highlight real business needs and inspire empathy.

For an example of this, let's look at Banner - University Medical Center, a hospital in Phoenix that recently completed a significant investment in their maternity ward, adding homelike private rooms and water laboring tubs:

- **The business goal.** One of Banner's business goals could have been to become known as a safer alternative to natural birthing centers and home births. They definitely want to show up when someone in Phoenix googles terms like "birth center tours" or "natural birthing Phoenix."
- **The emotions behind the search.** For an expecting parent, choosing where to give birth is typically a high-stress decision. During public-health crises (such as COVID-19), the stress surrounding that decision may be even higher: hospital visitor policies rapidly change, and in-person tours of birthing centers may be impossible. People who are anxious and dealing with an ambiguous situation are looking for reassurance and confidence.
- **The search demo.** A quick Google search for "tour birthing center phoenix az" reveals that Banner doesn't even show up on the first page of results. Dignity Health, a rival healthcare system, wins the top spot with a helpful, actionable search listing (**FIG 6.2**).

When demoing for your organization, throw your critical search queries into Google and show how your organization plays into the search engine results page:

- Where do you rank for those queries?
- Is the meta description clear and helpful?
- Does the content quickly address the search intent?
- Can you easily find the answer to your question?
- When visiting your site, do the navigation and functionality make it easy for someone to find related information?
- How quickly does the page load?
- Is there a clear call to action or path to conversion?
- Do your competitors do a better job at this than you do?

FIG 6.2: Dignity Health won the first organic search listing position in the SERP, and their listing provides a number to call for more information about when they hold tours.

Ask stakeholders to do this on their own, as well, so they can see firsthand how the user experience begins with search. Clearly, this is more impactful if you've found gaps in user experience and search intent that you could address ahead of time. Use this method strategically to highlight the need for investment in SEO.

Talk about the bottom line

Stakeholders are often unconcerned with SEO because they don't realize how much poor search visibility is costing them in actual dollars. Connecting search performance to fiscal performance can be an eye-opening and very persuasive tool.

There's no exact process for doing this; depending on your situation, some strategies might be more effective than others. There are two main angles you can take here.

If you're already getting a significant amount of traffic from organic search, but you know there's still room for improvement:

- First, do a little analytics homework to help people understand how organic search currently contributes to the site's overall traffic (percentage of total traffic and business outcomes).
- Next, compare how much organic search contributes to conversions relative to other marketing channels. If you have the data to assign a dollar value to those conversions, even better. For many organizations, organic search is one of the top contributors to conversions, if not the first. Why would you not set aside budget to protect and improve one of your top-performing site assets?
- Calculate the value organic search is bringing to your site already by using a search tool, like Ahrefs, to estimate what the *cost per click* (CPC) would be if that traffic came from paid search instead. Typically, the SEO investment you need to make will be modest compared to the amount you're already saving.

If getting traffic from organic search is currently a struggle and you know your site just isn't getting the baseline organic visibility your organization needs:

- Highlight your organic search weaknesses. The goal here is to paint a picture of the search opportunity compared to the organic traffic your site gets. Is there a significant gap between the estimated search traffic around how many people are already searching for products, services, or information like yours and the actual traffic from organic search your site gets? If this sounds like the situation you're facing, try one or more of the tools mentioned in the next step.
- Use a traffic-estimating tool (like Ahrefs, Semrush, or SpyFu) to gauge how your site stacks up in organic search against

your competitors' domains. This data, while only an estimate, can be compelling if it demonstrates that your competitors' sites are getting significantly more organic search visibility and traffic than yours. No one likes to underperform. Hard data can make the point that SEO is something your organization needs to address.

- Take a look at the conversions you're getting from organic search versus paid search campaigns, and then compare the budget you're putting into maintaining your website with how much you're investing in paid search. Sometimes it can be eye-opening to see how disproportionate the investment is, comparatively speaking.

- Look into your analytics platform to see if there has been a recent drop in traffic. If so, this can create a sense of urgency and a desire to get those numbers back up. If you're also tracking conversions in analytics, you can then compare the conversions from organic search from before and after the drop in traffic, which will likely also show a drop and help bolster your argument.

- Use Google Search Console to understand the level of nonbrand search traffic your site is currently getting. Remember, one of the main goals of SEO is to generate visibility for those who are unfamiliar with or not actively searching for the brand or organization name. Compare the relationship between nonbrand and brand search traffic levels to see how well you're accomplishing this goal.

With perseverance and due diligence, you can make a compelling case for SEO in your organization—and gain the support and budget you need to move forward. Like any endeavor worth your investment, you have to create space for it and ensure you have the support needed for it to thrive and become a priority; otherwise, it never becomes important enough to succeed. Let's take a look at the groundwork you need to do to make your SEO effort count.

INTEGRATING SEO INTO YOUR WORKFLOW

One of the best ways to sustain SEO buy-in and keep momentum going is to have a plan for how SEO will fit into your workflow on a practical level. As we've discussed throughout this book, SEO isn't just about using search data to optimize what you've got—it's about learning what people need by studying the way they search and then designing a web experience that meets those needs. This requires more SEO involvement earlier in the web design process.

Now that you understand what human-centered SEO takes, you're ready to apply what you've learned about integrating it into your workflow and create a plan to bring it all together.

It takes a village

As we discussed in Chapter 3, you'll need input, resources, and support from a diverse set of stakeholders to get human-centered SEO off the ground in your organization. This is especially true if you work in an organization unfamiliar with SEO.

Secure your stakeholders

Before you begin your search project, go back over the stakeholder roles identified in Chapter 3 and think about the people in your organization. Who's good at rallying support from leadership? Who's good at socializing research? Who's good at pulling together a cross-functional team? Once you've identified the people who might be able to help your project be successful, meet with them individually and discuss how they can be involved and what role they'll play.

Assemble the project team

SEO is an ongoing and sometimes challenging endeavor, because the people whose help you need to implement it are on different teams and work under different management. Without the help from even one of those resources, SEO can stall out indefinitely. In order to implement SEO recommendations, you'll need ongoing commitment from a cross-functional team, including whoever owns SEO in your organization now (if anyone), a designer, a developer, and a web writer—plus access to product managers and subject-matter experts, a project manager who understands resource allocation, and involvement from leadership who can bring such a team together. It's wise to set up a regularly occurring project stand-up meeting with these folks where they can discuss what they're working on, what they've learned, and any roadblocks standing in their way.

Project plan together

Clearly, integrating SEO takes collaboration. That's why project planning as a cross-functional team is so helpful when it comes to uniting SEO, content, design, and user experience—*especially* if there's tension between those roles or teams. We like to kick off every project, from big redesigns to relatively simple iterative site improvements, with a cross-functional project "roadmap" working session. During these sessions, we start with the project goal or end state and then ask the team to lay out all the work leading up to that end state.

A project roadmap typically includes:

- **Milestones.** These are specific points in time used to measure your progress toward the end goal—things like wrapping up research, completing the site architecture, or launching a page template.
- **Steps.** These are the straightforward steps between all of the milestones it takes to get the project done—steps like conducting user interviews, creating a site map or wireframes, or doing frontend development.
- **Tasks.** Individual tasks are the work required to complete each of the steps, sort of like substeps. So for "creating a site map," you might have tasks like "organize site content into new categories" or "determine nomenclature or labels," etc.
- **Interdependencies.** Once your team has laid out all of the steps and tasks it will take to do the work, you can identify areas of overlapping responsibility, shared tasks, or feedback

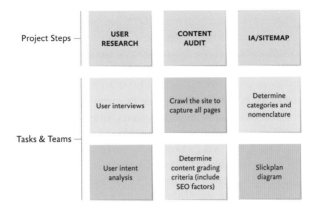

Project Steps	USER RESEARCH	CONTENT AUDIT	IA/SITEMAP
Tasks & Teams	User interviews	Crawl the site to capture all pages	Determine categories and nomenclature
	User intent analysis	Determine content grading criteria (include SEO factors)	Slickplan diagram

FIG 6.3: As we build out our project roadmaps, we designate different colors for each role on the project team to indicate which tasks each person or team is ultimately responsible for. In this example, the yellow stickies represent tasks owned by the content strategist, pink represents those owned by the SEO specialist, and purple belongs to the user experience designer. Color-coding like this makes it easier to see who's involved in each project phase at a glance.

loops needed to make sure an SEO perspective gets included when and where it needs to be.

We like to use sticky notes or a visualization tool like Miro to build out our project roadmaps (**FIG 6.3**).

You can use the resulting roadmap to build out a more detailed and formal project plan or Gantt chart. As a bonus, beyond making space for SEO, we've found that most everyone on the team appreciates this process and likes having more say in how their work intersects with other disciplines.

During these cross-functional planning sessions, you'll also want to ask:

- **Will you include search intent in the research phase of the project?** If so, how many topics will you research? How can you align the timing of that work with other research efforts so that all of the insights and recommendations have an opportunity to influence design?

- **How will you address SEO in your site's information architecture?** What are the next practical steps to involve one another in those areas? Do you need to book a one-on-one meeting with someone and plan out how you'll coordinate your work? Will this task be shared across teams or roles?
- **How will you align page content, templates, metadata, and user experience to search intent and to one another?** Will you do a content-planning exercise like we outlined in Chapter 4? Who would be involved in that? Who, ultimately, is responsible for doing the work in those areas?
- **What is your plan for carrying over SEO-friendly design decisions in development?** Will development be involved in a cross-functional SEO team? If not, what will the development handoff look like?

It can be awkward and messy to dive into all of the problems you might face as a team embarking on this work, but coming together to proactively identify potential collaboration and success roadblocks isn't only an exercise in humility—after all, you're admitting that something is bound to go wrong at some point—but it also helps you prepare for any issues that do arise.

MEASURING SUCCESS

We once worked with a company that came to us with an interesting problem. They had recently done a lot of organic search optimization work and, at first, it seemed like a smashing success—they'd increased organic traffic by 20 percent and everyone was pretty happy about it. At least they *were* happy, until they noticed the number of leads they were generating had dropped by 15 percent and the number of those leads that turned to real customers had dropped by 8 percent.

Doing a little digging, it became clear that the boost in traffic was from new content that was good at generating views— from people who didn't actually represent the target audience. Course-correcting would mean removing some of the "popular" content and changing key messages to better align with real prospective users.

But when it came time to make that shift, marketing leadership was scared to do it, if not downright hostile about it. Their team's success metrics and their *personal job performance* were tied to increased traffic. They weren't technically on the hook for increased leads and conversions—another team was. The culture at this organization wasn't flexible enough to change how they measured the website's success until the next fiscal year, so marketing leadership was incentivized to choose traffic over real business outcomes in order to protect their jobs.

Sadly, this happens all too often. But it doesn't have to be that way. Setting clear, achievable goals and having a plan for tracking their progress can make all the difference.

Identifying SEO goals

Having all the organic search traffic in the world won't matter if that traffic doesn't result in increased business outcomes. Your organization doesn't exist to get more traffic or to win at search rankings; it exists to serve a specific purpose. Whether your site is designed to collect donations, communicate regulations, or sell a product or service, organic search should help you achieve those goals.

When it comes to establishing goals for SEO, avoid chasing vanity metrics like increased rankings or traffic alone, as these can lead to weak and short-sighted strategy decisions. Instead, align your organic search performance metrics with key business initiatives at your organization, like:

- increased revenue
- increased enrollments
- increased leads and contact-form submissions
- increased donations
- subject-matter expertise
- a new product or service launch
- communication around a shift in key messaging
- new audience outreach

For each initiative or business outcome, brainstorm what trackable, tangible actions people could take on the website that would show evidence of the website contributing to that outcome. Those will be the conversions you can use to measure search performance.

Take General Electric, for example (http://bkaprt.com/ seo38/06-02). In 2014, they revamped their content strategy to align it with a global audience and engage the next generation of technology investors. They hired Tomas Kellner, who had been a staff writer at Forbes for eight years, to bring a journalistic approach to covering innovation and technology breakthroughs. They also launched GE Reports, the brand's content hub for stories revolving around the work done by General Electric in areas of tech, machinery, and advanced manufacturing. Clearly, driving engagement with this content and reaching the investor audience was a significant business initiative for GE.

Now, we're not sure how they ultimately tracked success for that project, but a smart SEO goal for them would have been to tie organic search performance to that initiative in an effort to increase traffic to the GE Reports content hub, ultimately driving more leads from the investor relations page that's linked to the site's navigation.

In applying such strategies to your own situation, you could make goals like this even more measurable and specific by setting performance targets based on existing analytics data and marketing projections.

Conversions

A *conversion* occurs when a visitor to your website completes a desired goal, like filling out a form, making a donation, or completing a purchase. You can put conversions into one of two categories—macro or micro—to track different actions and outcomes.

Macro conversions are the primary actions a user can take on your site that fulfill a business goal. They are typically monetary-based (driving increased profit or revenue) or lead-acquisition-based (generating leads for your organization). You can identify them relative to your business goals and metrics:

BUSINESS INITIATIVE	METRIC TO TRACK	SAMPLE MACRO CONVERSIONS
Reach new investors	Number of leads	Form fill on investor page
Increase revenue	Revenue	Order completions
Be known for specific subject matter	Number of event attendees	Webinar registration
Increase donations	Donations	Online donations

Be wary of establishing too many macro conversions. The more macro conversions you have, the more work you'll need to do to estimate and prioritize their value. Keep things simple and trackable by choosing three to four key metrics that are most closely tied to revenue or business outcomes.

Micro conversions are all of the interactions a user can take on your site that could lead to a macro conversion. They are typically either *navigation-based* (visiting certain sections or pages of your site), or *interaction-based* (using features on your site). It's important to track these in order to identify areas of the site (or specific content, features, or functionality) that play a direct role in generating macro conversions.

What micro conversions look like:

- reading an article
- using an interactive tool
- visiting a key page on the site
- watching a video
- signing up for a newsletter
- downloading a white paper

Let's go back to the GE example for a moment. If their business initiative was to drive engagement with future investors through the GE Reports content hub, their macro conversions could look like a form fill on the investor page, tracked by the number of leads that page generates. And their micro conversions would be things like organic traffic visits to articles on GE Reports, watching videos embedded in the articles, or newsletter sign-ups.

Since micro conversions aren't revenue-based, you shouldn't use them to measure business success—but you *can and should* use them as indicators that users are heading in the right direction, or to develop a better understanding of where things might be going wrong.

They say that if you can't measure it, you can't improve it. Establish macro and micro conversions collaboratively with key stakeholders across your organization so there's consensus about how everyone involved defines and measures success.

Behavioral and site performance metrics

Beyond establishing and tracking your macro and micro goals, you'll want to keep an eye on metrics in your analytics platform to help you gauge how traffic is coming to your site, how long visitors stay, and how they're interacting with your content. It's important to remember that metrics are not goals; they're just tools you can use to learn about how users experience your website. You don't have to go overboard here—it's best to stick to the essentials. The metrics you'll want to include in your report are:

- **Site traffic.** Watch out for dramatic dips or downward trends in traffic. This could mean something's going wrong and you need to try to figure out why, or it could signal what content is driving the loss or gain in visibility and how you can correct any issues. On the flip side, if things are trending upward or there are dramatic gains in traffic, you'll want to learn what content is driving that increase and if there's anything you can do to keep the positive results rolling in.
- **Bounce rate.** You may recall that a bounce is simply a visit to your site where the user does not visit any other pages in that session—regardless of how long they stayed on the page they visited. It's a very neutral metric that literally does not mean anything positive or negative on its own. Bounce rates mean different things for different types of content. Define what a single page session means to your organization, or

even to just specific types of pages on your site, and monitor those over time. A dramatic increase or decrease could mean something's off.

- **Time on site.** As with bounce rates, time on site is completely contextual, based on your site's content and what it's designed to do. For some folks, less time can mean you've clarified your site experience and people can find what they need faster; for others, it can mean you removed in-depth content people actually wanted and so they're leaving. The key thing here is that when you make changes to your site content, you need to understand what changes in time on site mean for that content and keep track of it over time. One thing to watch out for is time on site in comparison with page views. Shorter time coupled with high page views can mean users aren't finding what they need (rapidly going from page to page without time to really digest the content). If you notice this, investigate the user flow and look for any issues.

  Alternatively, you could use some handy code created by Dana DiTomaso of Kickpoint that tracks a blend of these metrics she calls *content consumption*. You can insert this Google Analytics script through Google Tag Manager; it will allow you to track whether visitors stay long enough on a page to read your content and whether they scroll far enough down the page to actually see all your content (http://bkaprt.com/seo38/06-03).

Beyond monitoring overall site performance, if your URLs are consistent, clear, and reflect the structure of your site, you'll be able to drill down by section to gauge relative performance for that group of related pages. The most common, and useful, forms of segmentation to measure include:

- **Types of content or sections.** This helps you understand how different areas of your website (specific topics, products, or services) are performing, and how people interact with various content types.
- **Landing page traffic.** Keep an eye out for pages with high traffic from organic search. Pages like that are typically get-

ting search visibility and they might be the very first page on your site someone sees, so you want to optimize them accordingly. Likewise, if you notice unusually low traffic on any pages you've deemed important to organic search, you can flag them for investigation and improvement. URLs with high organic traffic numbers can also indicate content that's important to users and present an opportunity to expand on that content.

- **Regions or languages.** This segmentation allows you to see how your regional or language-targeted sites are performing.
- **Channels.** You'll want to be able to see site reporting for traffic coming from sources outside of organic search, like direct visitors, paid search traffic, social media referrals, and email.

REPORTING

Keeping an eye on how your site is performing in organic search and communicating that performance to stakeholders is critical to the success of your SEO strategy.

With search algorithms and SERP design constantly evolving, performance for any website can fluctuate at a moment's notice. Reporting not only tips you off to fluctuations, but also allows you to understand how your optimization efforts tie back to your organization's business goals. SEO reports should provide an overview of how a website is performing in organic search, focusing on behavioral metrics, organic traffic, and whether or not that traffic is leading to macro and micro conversions.

We typically recommend creating at least two types of reports: one for leadership (with a focus on key metrics), and one that's more of a diagnostic deep dive (where you screen for any problems and make sure all is well). Now, let's look at how to capture and report the data for those metrics.

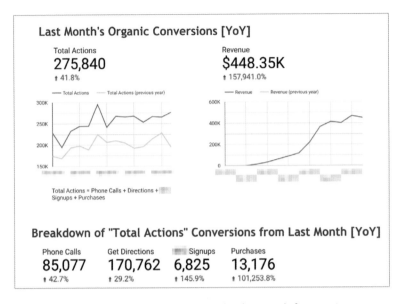

FIG 6.4: A report from Google Data Studio, tailored in this example for executives to reveal how organic search is performing against this organization's macro conversions (such as phone calls, purchases, and getting directions).

Reporting tools

We've recommended spreadsheets for nearly every document in this book, but we won't do that here. Avoid static formats like Excel for your reporting template; manually updating data in spreadsheets is a huge time suck that will pull you away from more impactful work.

Luckily, there are plenty of reporting tools to choose from. Our favorite free tool is Google Data Studio, which provides a dynamic, automatically updating interface that ties into other data sources like Google Analytics, paid ad data, and more (**FIG 6.4**).

Other data-visualization tools, like Tableau and Power BI, can be costly to set up and manage over time, so unless your organization has very ambitious and tightly integrated tracking metrics and business goals, you probably don't need them.

Whatever tool you choose, it will have all of the base functionality required to track goals and performance metrics, but you'll still need to customize the tool's reporting dashboard to make it meaningful for your organization. You should set it up clearly so that any stakeholder will be able to immediately understand how the site is performing against its most important business outcomes.

Most reporting tools will allow you to configure different tabs that report on different metrics. This is where our recommendation of building at least two reporting tabs—one for executives and one for diagnostics—comes into play.

Tab #1: The executive summary

Your ongoing SEO reporting for executives should include macro and micro conversions, trended data over time, and percent changes in performance (year-over-year or month-over-month). Whatever conversion data you ultimately include in your executive summary report tab, this data should:

- facilitate conversation by giving stakeholders from different teams a chance to regroup and make adjustments collaboratively, and
- help track progress on goals and prove the value of SEO to key stakeholders on an ongoing basis—enhancing their buy-in.

Tab #2: The detailed diagnostics

In addition to your executive summary tab that keeps track of conversion data, your deep-dive diagnostic should monitor behavioral data, site performance metrics, and performance for different page types or specific types of content. The detailed diagnostic section of your report should:

- enable better, quicker decision-making by establishing baselines and catching extreme search performance fluctuations when they happen, and

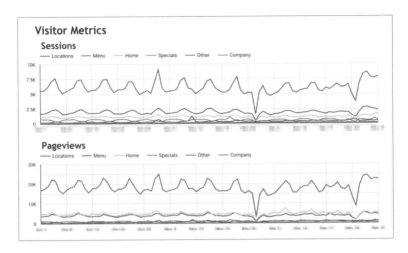

FIG 6.5: This reporting template for a restaurant chain website has been segmented by page type, making it easy to quickly tell which page types, or sections of the site, perform the best and drive the most macro and micro conversions.

- help the team truly understand when and why your SEO efforts are working.

For example, you could summarize the performance for all URLs in a specific section or type of page (**FIG 6.5**). Summing up this data helps you understand how each page type contributes to the site total (in terms of traffic, conversions, and UX metrics) and how your optimizations impact each type of content.

Bear in mind that reports alone lack context around strategy and ongoing work. When you share performance reports, give executives the context they need to make sense of them, and keep team members in the loop on upcoming work they might want to weigh in on by including progress reports. These should list upcoming projects with expected launch dates, explanations of each initiative, and the anticipated impact on search ranking and the user experience, as well as recently completed tasks with their completion dates and the actual results of the work.

Reporting frequency

Review your report on a monthly basis with key team members and SEO stakeholders. Depending on your company culture and organizational SEO literacy, this can be as formal as a presentation with a polished deck (for those who need more context and explanation), or as modest as an in-depth email (for folks who are comfortable with analytics data and how it ties into your SEO strategy). A monthly cadence is ideal: it gives your optimizations the chance to take effect, and you'll still catch issues with enough time to do something about them.

Outside of the monthly report, have at least one member of the team check in on performance on a weekly basis. This will help you catch any major fluctuations in close to real time. You can set up alerts in your analytics platform to quickly catch a spike or decline that needs attention. Any time you see a dramatic increase or decrease in traffic or conversions, you need to know why. Maybe something you've recently implemented on the site has gone wrong, like a pop-up ad that's misfiring and blocking users from interacting with your site—and quickly removing it solves the problem as soon as it started. Other shifts, like a drop in traffic because you're in the middle of a pandemic and people simply don't have the bandwidth to pay as much attention to your product or service, might not be such quick fixes. Whatever the reason, a positive or negative spike in traffic is always cause for investigation so that you can change your strategy if necessary.

However frequently you review your reports, it's important to compare the previous snapshot in time of the site's performance to the most current view. That way, you can catch any increase or losses in traffic over time. If seasonality matters to your organization, reviewing the data from a previous season compared to the current one (or year-over-year) helps you put gains or losses in traffic in perspective with any seasonal patterns.

Communicating results

It's wise to set low expectations for the first month or two after migration or launch because Google needs time to follow

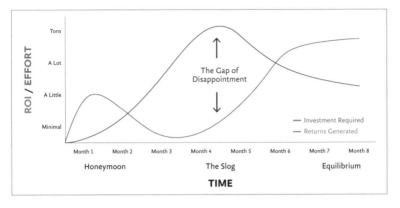

FIG 6.6: This graph from Moz explains how the benefits of implementing SEO best practices in an organization can take several months and involve a lengthy period of diminishing returns (http://bkaprt.com/seo38/06-04).

redirects and get used to new internal linking structures, pages, and content. During this initial time period, it's pretty normal to see a decline in search engine visibility. In some cases, you might see positive results right away, but in most cases, it can take three to four months to start seeing your work pay off.

Regardless of site migrations or launches, sometimes you put in a lot of SEO work in general and, for whatever reason, it just doesn't pay off or, even worse, organic traffic or business outcomes take a dive. Don't lose heart. There are myriad reasons for issues like this—anything from slow crawlers to implementation mishaps to fluctuations in algorithm updates (**FIG 6.6**).

On the other hand, if your traffic problems are persistent, you may need more technical SEO expertise to help you troubleshoot the cause. In the meantime, when you have to share negative results with your team, remember to:

- Reiterate the business and SEO goals related to your current project.
- State when the work started and (if applicable) when the site launched or migration was completed.
- Explain the numbers. Include the date range for data you are sharing and what timeframe you're comparing it to.

- Avoid placing blame on individuals or teams for weak search rankings. Remind stakeholders that strong search rankings come from collaborative, multidisciplinary work over time.
- Identify any strategic changes you recommend in response to the results. Remember: little optimizations become more impactful in aggregate—over time, small efforts can add up to larger gains.

Your company's reporting is more than a set of metrics—it's a powerful tool that allows you to understand where user needs are being met and how your site is contributing to the overall goals of your organization. Done right, your reporting template can act as a North Star that keeps everyone working together toward meaningful search visibility and improved site performance.

ONWARD

Doing SEO right means you will be competing for extra resources and funding dollars; you'll have to rely on the relationships you've built and the knowledge you've gained.

Just ask Daryl Hemeon, a marketing technologist at Unum Group. A few years ago, when he helped lead a site redesign at his organization, Hemeon knew SEO would be a critical part of reaching the company's goals—but it wasn't easy convincing leadership to make the investment. In the end, it was his careful preparation that won them over. As he told us during a phone interview:

> The reason we got the funding came down to three things: the business case was strong, we had a plan that showed we knew what we were doing, and most importantly we did a good job educating people on the need for SEO in the first place.

Once he won the budget, Hemeon made sure the team had a plan to measure and communicate success from the very start. And now, you've got the tools to make that happen, too.

CONCLUSION

AT THE OUTSET OF THIS BOOK, we said that making sure content is findable isn't just the responsibility of people with SEO in their job title, but rather the collective responsibility of people just like you—the designers, content specialists, developers, and project managers of the world. Without you, human-centered SEO simply cannot happen.

You've got what it takes

Including search data and SEO considerations in the design process is just the first step. Most of the time, people have no problem getting the data and tools necessary to make SEO happen, but they confront organizational and business roadblocks to implementing the very changes that will deliver real results.

Adding that new page to the site, changing the language in the main navigation, addressing content gaps in a user-centric way—this kind of work takes buy-in and collaboration. Successfully pulling off SEO is just as much about wrangling people as it is about wrangling technical tweaks and words on the page. It requires looking at organic search differently and then changing the way we approach design because of that new perspective. If you're reading the conclusion to this book, you're probably part of that change already.

Algorithms change, but human-centered design stays the same

Meanwhile, while you're busy changing perspectives, search algorithms are also changing. Today, Google sets the bar for how we use search, but tomorrow? Who knows how the search landscape will change? Every other year or so, someone proclaims that SEO is dead. We predict that the practice of search optimization isn't going anywhere, but the line between what you do for search engines and what you do for people *is* fading away. The secret to a search strategy that holds up over the long term is this: when we stay focused on what matters to our users, we'll be ready for whatever technology and time bring our way.

The tools you use to analyze search data will evolve, and new tools that are even better at parsing user intent from raw search data are sure to emerge, but the principles of sound user research will remain the same. Just remember that search data is really people data. As long as you make space to spend time with that data to uncover what people are saying about what they want and need, and address those needs through content and design, you'll be on the right track—no matter how algorithms and search engines change.

How you approach SEO is about more than just showing up in search results. It's a reflection of your organization's values and a deliberate choice about what you will be found and known for. When it comes to human-centered search optimization, the key is to build sites that are manageable, technically sound, and performant—and, above all else, to do what's right for the very real people searching in the first place.

ACKNOWLEDGMENTS

To our readers. Thank you for having an open mind and letting go of any preconceived notions you may have had about SEO—and thanks for taking a chance on this book. We're thrilled you care enough to invest in human-centered search, and to invest in yourselves. Go forth and make SEO part of your design workflow. You got this!

To Lisa Maria Marquis and Katel LeDû. Thank you for believing in us, and for believing in the idea that design work would benefit users more if it were designed with search insights in mind. We are so grateful for your unbelievable patience and encouragement. To Lisa Maria (yes, again), we're in awe of your editing prowess, the way you balance kindness and candor, your impressive ability to turn our messy ideas into something coherent and, dare we say, helpful? We'd ask you to come edit our whole life, but there's no way we could afford that. To Caren Litherland, your edits always had a magical way of making us feel seen. To Mat Marquis, you're brilliant, okay? You pack more personality into one Word doc comment than most people could pump into an entire novel. Thanks for holding our thoughts on technical SEO up to your rigorous, no-nonsense development standards.

To our family—Melissa, Matt, Virginia, Pomar, and Bodie. Thank you for your extreme patience and support while we spent a gazillion hours on weekends and late nights working on the book. You did more than your fair share of stuff around the house, suffered through boring weekends at home, put up with our moods, and loved us so well throughout the entire process. Sorry for all the times we were preoccupied and only half-present. You're the best partners, kiddo, and fur babies anyone could hope to have. Let's go to the park and book all those vacations now!

To our parents—Barbara, Bill, Cathy, and Ron. We wrote a (brief) book! Not bad, right? You and your stellar child-rearing are entirely responsible for this. Thanks for instilling in us the value of hard work, curiosity, and doing the right thing no matter what. You taught us to question established norms and speak up when it counts—two traits that have certainly served us well in making SEO better. Hopefully, reading this will finally give you a clearer picture of what we do all day.

To Victoria and Anabelle. Thanks for all the sister solidarity, free babysitting, late-night calls, love, and encouragement.

To Dana DiTomaso and Mike Corak, our wonderful peer reviewers. Thank you for being so generous with your time and expertise. It was unbelievably valuable for us to be able to bounce ideas off other experts for feedback. And to Mike, thanks for just being the raddest big bro anyone could ever have.

To Jonathon Colman, Dr. Pete Myers, Sarah Winters, Rand Fishkin, and Dan Shure. Your work has had such a profound impact on ours. Thank you for letting us learn from you and for giving a damn about the work you do. Lastly, thanks for sharing so generously of your time and expertise with us during the development of this book.

To Kristina Halvorson, you're just the best. Thanks for all you've given to the content community. Thank you for having faith in us, and for letting us sneak a little bit about SEO into Confab from time to time. To Sara Wachter-Boettcher, endless gratitude. Thanks for inviting us to the table, for cheering us on, and for being a constant badass and inspiration.

To our clients past and present. Thanks for trusting us, thanks for bringing us into your organizations and giving us room to do things a little differently. And most of all, thanks for letting us learn so, so much from you and your teams. We consider the work we do alongside you all to be a real privilege.

To Bret Giles and Margie Traylor, thanks for your confidence in us and for creating the space where we could meet and make exciting things happen. And to all of our magnificent friends, former coworkers, and comrades—you've made us better in many ways and we're so grateful for your knowledge, support, and collaboration.

RESOURCES

WE HOPE WE'VE WHETTED your appetite for diving into SEO—
and if you're hungry for more, we couldn't be more pleased. In
this section are our recommendations to help you deepen your
knowledge, expand your repertoire, and continue the journey
into human-centered search.

SEO 101

- Get familiar with Google's Search Quality Raters Guidelines
  (http://bkaprt.com/seo38/02-04, PDF).
- Learn organic search fundamentals with Moz's free SEO
  Learning Center (http://bkaprt.com/seo38/07-01).
- Understand how Google's algorithm has evolved over time
  and what it means for websites with Moz's "Google Algorithm Update History: A History of Major Google Algorithm Updates from 2000–Present" (http://bkaprt.com/
  seo38/07-02).

Technical SEO

- Dive deeper into technical SEO with Google's SEO Starter
  Guide (http://bkaprt.com/seo38/07-03).
- Explore the full list of Schema.org structured data types
  (http://bkaprt.com/seo38/04-07).
- Read Google's structured data guidelines (http://bkaprt.com/
  seo38/05-15).
- Get Mike King's take on how technical SEO works under
  the hood (http://bkaprt.com/seo38/05-18).
- Understand JavaScript's role in SEO and find out how to
  implement it in a search-friendly way (http://bkaprt.com/
  seo38/05-07).
- Learn what to consider when you're working with hreflang
  and international SEO, and discover a very helpful implementation guide (http://bkaprt.com/seo38/07-04).
- Configure analytics to more accurately report content consumption within a page (http://bkaprt.com/seo38/06-03).

Tools of the trade

- Google's URL Inspector Tool, XML sitemap submission, index coverage, Core Web Vitals, and mobile usability reporting help you see which keywords are generating visibility for your site in Google and how your pages are crawled and indexed (http://bkaprt.com/seo38/07-05).
- Screaming Frog SEO Spider helps you improve SEO by extracting data and auditing for common issues (http://bkaprt.com/seo38/07-06).
- Use Semrush and Ahrefs for keyword research, competitive research for traffic and links, rank tracking, and ongoing crawl audits (http://bkaprt.com/seo38/07-07).
- Use Moz for keyword and link research, rank tracking, and ongoing crawl audits (http://bkaprt.com/seo38/07-08, http://bkaprt.com/seo38/07-09).
- Google Trends gives you access to search data trended over time by topic or keyword—especially useful for understanding subject matter growth (and decline) in search demand (http://bkaprt.com/seo38/07-10).
- Google's Core Web Vitals initiative helps you see site speed and website performance related to overall user experience (http://bkaprt.com/seo38/05-08).
- Validate your Schema.org implementation with this structured data-testing tool (http://bkaprt.com/seo38/07-11).
- Visualize design decisions and collaborate with folks around content, UX, and SEO remotely in real time with Miro (http://bkaprt.com/seo38/07-12).
- User Interviews helps you recruit participants quickly and affordably (http://bkaprt.com/seo38/07-13).
- Optimal Workshop's Treejack lets you test your information architecture with real people to see where and why folks might get lost when searching for your content (http://bkaprt.com/seo38/07-14).

SEO news and blogs

- Search Engine Roundtable covers the most interesting threads taking place in search engine marketing forums (http://bkaprt.com/seo38/07-15).
- Search Engine Land brings you breaking stories, industry trends, feature announcements, and product changes at popular platforms used by search professionals (http://bkaprt.com/seo38/07-16).
- On the Moz blog, industry experts offer their best advice, research, how-tos, and SEO insights (http://bkaprt.com/seo38/07-17).
- SEO by the Sea explores search-related patents and papers with a perspective on how they could impact SEO (http://bkaprt.com/seo38/07-18).

Design and collaboration resources

- Stanford dSchool has some of our favorite resources and templates for thinking and working better, together—which is super important if you're running a meeting or workshop that considers the intersection of content, UX, and SEO (http://bkaprt.com/seo38/07-19).
- *Gamestorming* is a very useful set of design-thinking and cocreation tools and templates to help you innovate and collaborate effectively (http://bkaprt.com/seo38/07-20).
- IDEO's Design Kit platform hosts human-centered design resources, case studies, methodologies, and more (http://bkaprt.com/seo38/07-21).
- 18F, the US Government's design consultancy, has created a comprehensive set of user-centered design principles and standards (http://bkaprt.com/seo38/07-22).

REFERENCES

Shortened URLs are numbered sequentially; the related long URLs are listed below for reference.

Chapter 1

01-01   https://www.searchenginejournal.com/seo-101/seo-statistics/

01-02   https://gs.statcounter.com/search-engine-market-share#monthly-201712-201812-bar

01-03   https://www.webfx.com/blog/seo/2019-search-market-share/

01-04   https://moz.com/beginners-guide-to-seo/how-search-engines-operate

01-05   https://developers.google.com/search/docs/advanced/guidelines/webmaster-guidelines

01-06   https://webmasters.googleblog.com/2011/05/more-guidance-on-building-high-quality.html

01-07   https://blog.google/products/search/search-language-understanding-bert/

01-08   https://developers.google.com/search/mobile-sites/mobile-first-indexing

Chapter 2

02-01   https://www.seroundtable.com/google-says-as-search-engines-get-better-at-intent-keyword-research-wont-go-away-28810.html

02-02   https://twitter.com/dan_shure/status/1169735619054112769

02-03   https://www.cis.upenn.edu/~nenkova/Courses/cis430/p3-broder.pdf

02-04   https://static.googleusercontent.com/media/guidelines.raterhub.com/en//searchqualityevaluatorguidelines.pdf

02-05   https://support.google.com/webmasters/answer/9008080?hl=en

02-06   https://ahrefs.com/blog/long-tail-keywords/

Chapter 3

03-01   https://www.braintraffic.com/blog/the-secrets-to-stakeholder-alignment

03-02   https://docs.google.com/spreadsheets/d/1KpYJq3mEQvRHQqDRlx7Z1w-ZWVkXraNMvUN2m3UNFNEo/edit?usp=sharing

Chapter 4

04-01   https://contentdesign.london/content-design/search-engine-optimisation-seo-and-content/

04-02   https://www.usability.gov/what-and-why/information-architecture.html

04-03 https://www.seobythesea.com/2016/04/googles-reasonable-surfer-patent-updated/

04-04 https://alistapart.com/article/the-core-model-designing-inside-out-for-better-results/

04-05 https://twitter.com/johnmu/status/980902538865205248

04-06 https://searchengineland.com/spammy-structured-markup-penalty-recovery-use-schema-markup-caution-223289

04-07 https://schema.org/docs/full.html

04-08 https://sparktoro.com/blog/new-jumpshot-2018-data-where-searches-happen-on-the-web-google-amazon-facebook-beyond

04-09 https://www.nngroup.com/articles/concise-scannable-and-objective-how-to-write-for-the-web/

04-10 https://www.semrush.com/blog/eat-and-ymyl-new-google-search-guidelines-acronyms-of-quality-content/

04-11 https://www.botify.com/blog/content-freshness-ranking-factor

Chapter 5

05-01 https://www.polemicdigital.com/perfecting-xml-sitemaps/

05-02 https://ahrefs.com/blog/canonical-tags/

05-03 https://uxplanet.org/4-ux-friendly-alternatives-to-infinite-scroll-8b486992183b

05-04 https://developers.google.com/search/blog/2014/02/infinite-scroll-search-friendly

05-05 http://scrollsample.appspot.com/items

05-06 https://www.searchpilot.com/resources/blog/split-testing-javascript-for-seo/

05-07 https://www.onely.com/blog/ultimate-guide-javascript-seo/

05-08 https://web.dev/vitals

05-09 https://web.dev/lcp/#what-is-a-good-lcp-score

05-10 https://web.dev/fid/#what-is-a-good-fid-score

05-11 https://web.dev/cls/#layout-shift-score

05-12 https://developers.google.com/speed/pagespeed/insights/

05-13 https://searchengineland.com/technical-seo-in-the-wild-real-world-issues-and-fixes-308578

05-14 https://developers.google.com/search/reference/overview

05-15 https://developers.google.com/search/docs/guides/sd-policies

05-16 https://www.w3.org/Provider/Style/URI.html

05-17 https://moz.com/learn/seo/redirection

05-18 https://moz.com/blog/the-technical-seo-renaissance
05-19 https://support.google.com/webmasters/answer/6033086?hl=en

Chapter 6

06-01 https://www.marketingprofs.com/podcasts/2016/30155/content-ux-tracy-rosecrans-heathline-marketing-smarts
06-02 https://digitaluncovered.com/inside-ges-content-startegy
06-03 https://kickpoint.ca/digital-content-marketing-analysis/
06-04 https://moz.com/blog/surviving-the-seo-slog-whiteboard-friday

Resources

07-01 https://moz.com/learn/seo
07-02 https://moz.com/google-algorithm-change
07-03 https://developers.google.com/search/docs/beginner/seo-starter-guide
07-04 https://www.onely.com/blog/ultimate-guide-javascript-seo
07-05 https://www.aleydasolis.com/en/search-engine-optimization/avoiding-hreflang-issues-by-following-a-6-steps-implementation-process/
07-06 https://search.google.com/search-console/about
07-07 https://www.screamingfrog.co.uk/seo-spider/
07-08 https://www.semrush.com
07-09 https://ahrefs.com
07-10 https://moz.com
07-11 https://trends.google.com/trends/
07-12 https://search.google.com/structured-data/testing-tool/u/0/
07-13 https://miro.com/app/dashboard/
07-14 https://www.userinterviews.com/
07-15 https://www.optimalworkshop.com/treejack/
07-16 https://www.seroundtable.com
07-17 https://searchengineland.com
07-18 https://moz.com/blog
07-19 https://www.seobythesea.com
07-20 https://dschool.stanford.edu
07-21 https://gamestorming.com/
07-22 https://www.designkit.org/
07-23 https://18f.gsa.gov/guides/

INDEX

ABOUT A BOOK APART

We cover the emerging and essential topics in web design and development with style, clarity, and above all, brevity—because working designer-developers can't afford to waste time.

COLOPHON

The text is set in FF Yoga and its companion, FF Yoga Sans, both by Xavier Dupré. Headlines and cover are set in Titling Gothic by David Berlow.

 This book was printed in the United States using FSC certified papers.